VEDANTA IN PRACTICE

Published by
The Secretary
The Ramakrishna Mission Institute of Culture
Calcutta-700 029, India

First Edition : March 2001
Second Print : March 2010 : 3000
Total Impression : 5000

Price in India : Rupees forty only

ISBN 81-87332-14-X

Printed in India
Computer typeset at
The Ramakrishna Mission Institute of Culture
Photo-offset at
Pelican Press
85, B. B. Ganguly Street
Kolkata - 700 012

VEDANTA IN PRACTICE

SWAMI LOKESWARANANDA

THE RAMAKRISHNA MISSION INSTITUTE OF CULTURE
GOL PARK, CALCUTTA 700 029

VEDANTA IN PRACTICE

CONTENTS

enduring ability to give human beings hope and courage in all circumstances, as well as strength to cope with the many challenges of life. This is exactly what these short essays by Swami Lokeswaranandaji aim for and achieve. We believe this book will be well received.

9 March 2001   **Swami Prabhananda**

PREFACE

From November 1975 to December 1998 Swami Lokeswaranandaji wrote the editorials, entitled *Observations*, for the *Bulletin* of the Ramakrishna Mission Institute of Culture [published up to February 1999]. These essays, each brief and self-contained, were topical and thought-provoking and aroused much interest among the reading public when they first appeared. Two anthologies of his *Observations* were published during his lifetime under the titles *Practical Spirituality* and *Religion and Culture*, and both of these books were highly appreciated. Both of them have already been reprinted more than once. His remaining *Observations* have now been compiled, and the result is this book, *Vedanta in Practice.*

Aware of the dichotomy between precept and practice in the religious life of people, particularly in India, Swami Lokeswaranandaji made use of his facile pen to guide people to the right path and also help them deal with the seemingly insurmountable obstacles of daily life. The essays in *Vedanta in Practice* are written in a popular style and cover a wide variety of topics, yet invariably they come round to the same point—that the goal of human life is to realize God and that human beings are in essence divine.

Needless to say, the word 'Vedanta' has been used in the title in a broad sense, for in this sense Vedanta has an

LOVE MEANS SACRIFICE

What is religion? Religion means love and forgiveness. Love everybody, no matter who he or she is, and no matter what offence he or she has committed against you. Christ says if someone hits you on the right cheek, give your left cheek also. This kind of forgiveness, however, requires a lot of courage and strength of mind. You can behave like this only when you have the right outlook on the world, when you know that no one is your enemy. This is the sum and substance of religion.

First love God. If you love God you would certainly not want to do anything which God forbids. You will not, for instance, hurt anybody. And you will try your best to love and forgive everybody. That is True Religion.

We make a lot of fuss about one religion and another. But if we look closely we find there is no difference. All religions preach more or less the same thing—Truth and forgiveness. In essence they are all One. If there is any difference, the difference is in details and rituals. And if you are truly religious, truly a Hindu, a Christian, or a Mohammedan, you will follow those principles.

When you worship Christ, you are worshipping God Himself. You are not worshipping a sectarian God. Christ was God Himself. We love Christ. We are grateful to Christ because of the sacrifice he made. In order to demonstrate to what extent he would go in forgiving others, he said at the time of crucifixion, 'Forgive them, O Lord, for they do not know what they are doing.' Why did Christ die that way? For our sake, for the sake of humanity.

Thus, crucifixion is the symbol of the extent of sacrifice you have to make for God. You say you love God. But can you prove it? If you say you love God truly, you would love to die for Him, or sacrifice anything you have. It is not that God wants you to sacrifice, but you, on your own, would like to sacrifice whatever you have for the sake of God. Take the case of Ramakrishna. Did Mother Kali ever say to him, 'Pick up the sword and kill yourself for My sake?' No. But Ramakrishna was about to do it.

Love means sacrifice. Even in normal human relationships love means sacrifice. You are happy to be able to sacrifice for the person you love. More so, in the case of God. I would love to give up everything for the sake of God whom I love. If you love God, you love everybody, because God loves you and He also loves all your fellow men and women. It is not that God loves you only. He loves all His children and looks after them. Do not say, 'I love God and therefore God loves me, and the best way to love God is the way I follow.' No. Religion is what you feel, how deeply you love your God. You need not demonstrate your love for God. Love and pray within yourself. And if you are praying deeply, tears will come to your eyes in spite of yourself. You do not want anybody to know that you are shedding tears. But because you love God deeply, tears will come to your eyes. This happens not only to you, a Hindu, but also to him, a Muslim, or to him, a Buddhist.

How to pray? One thing is certain. If you love God with all your heart and soul, your words and your language do not matter. God sees your heart and feeling. A baby cannot correctly pronounce 'mother' or 'father'. But the child's mother or father understands who he is addressing.

THREE HUNDRED YEARS OF A PARADOX

Though, perhaps euphemistically, Calcutta has been called a 'City of Joy', its hardships with contrasting charms make it a fascinating paradox. To call it a city is a joke; in reality, it is nothing but a sprawling slum. But what a slum !

To name some of its contrasts, here man and animal share the same pavement; millionaires and beggars live cheek by jowl; the most sophisticated and the most simple agitate together for a common cause. Here people from all over India come to work, for no other place offers opportunity such as this most ugly and ill-maintained city does. Those who so come start by hating everything they find in Calcutta—its filth, noise, and crowds. They are particularly disgusted with the tall claims the Bengalis make about their culture. But before long love replaces their hatred. They happen to discover the surprising charms Calcutta hides within its bosom.

What are these charms ? One only feels them. The first surprise that awaits you coming from outside is the treatment of the local people : you are welcome. No one in fact asks who you are, where you are from, and why you are in Calcutta. People just accept you. They may not feel happy that you are depriving one of them of his rightful claim to the job you are doing, but they never express that feeling. If they had any reservations at first, they now think you are one of them. You may have had some reservations yourself about the people around yourself, but before you know what is happening, you find yourself a member of the local committee of citizens for socio-

religious activities in the neighbourhood and you become
an inalienable part of the social scene. You are no more an
alien, you are one of the people. If you still have any
hesitancy, your children help you overcome it. They speak
the language of the State, they go to the same school as the
local children, they belong to the city more than the one
their parents came from, which they know little of and
have perhaps never visited. These children grow up and
find work in the city. In the process their roots go deeper
into the soil. Emotionally and otherwise, they are no
longer different from the children of the soil. Calcutta is
home to them as it is to all other ethnic groups. Calcutta is
totally cosmopolitan.

The story of how Calcutta grew is well known. A
handful of fortune seekers from the West landed on a
patch of marshy land on the river Hooghly (Ganga) way
back in the eighteenth century. They came to trade, but
soon found themselves in the role of empire builders. By
hook or by crook, they conquered the whole land. They
developed Calcutta to suit their needs, but only that much
and not more. They built a few magnificent buildings for
administrative purposes and for their own use, perhaps to
overawe the poor natives. The natives huddled together in
the surrounding slums, dying of epidemics or surviving
precariously. What did it matter to the rulers ?

Yet Calcutta grew and is still growing. During her
brief three hundred years of existence, she has nurtured
many great men and women including even an avatar. She
has also witnessed great social and political upheavals
which have finally swept the alien rulers out of the land.
Calcutta is always restless, either doing something original
or something totally irrational. Full of contradictions, she
is neither good nor bad, she is just a paradox.

A DREAM YET TO BE FULFILLED

For long, man has dreamt of a world order which will guarantee freedom, equality, and justice to all. That dream is yet to be fulfilled. After the First World War, the League of Nations was set up in the hope that it would usher in the change the world needed. It did not. Then the Second World War broke out. It was a trauma in which the entire human race was involved. When it ended everybody felt relieved. Once again, the cry went out for a world order that would rule out war once and for all. When the United Nations came into being, people hailed it, hoping this was a prelude to what they were looking for. Its working has since belied their hope. What is wrong with it ? Like the old League of Nations, it too is completely dominated by the Big Powers so that the interests of the smaller nations tend to be ignored. The selfishness of the Big Powers has practically defeated the purpose of the United Nations. There has been no major war yet, but the threat of it is always there. And if there is a war, which, happily, no one wants, it will be the end of everything. Some discerning people say even if there is no war, war-like conditions prevail, causing the same anxiety and tension as if a war is actually on. There is an all-pervasive sense of insecurity in the world today which keeps haunting man. Where is the relief that the United Nations promised?

The basic problem is in the attitude of the Big Powers. They do not realize that they are not for themselves only, they are also for the whole world. They have to uplift those who are less fortunate among the nations. History

shows that the strong invariably exploit and never care to
protect the weak. The law of the jungle still prevails. The
Big Powers might have led the world towards a moral
revolution, instead they have been busy settling political
disputes among themselves. They wrangle over their own
rights and privileges, but never think of sharing them with
others. The problem before man is not political, but moral.
It is a question of how much you are prepared to surrender
to help others. It is a question of what importance you
attach to virtues like compassion, justice, honesty, love,
and goodwill towards others. Leaders of the world are
those who represent the Big Powers. They have to be
people who are morally perfect, else they cannot lead and
inspire others.

The world is filled with selfishness and greed, hatred
and jealousy, dishonesty and crookedness. How can there
be a successful United Nations unless those who run it are
men and women of a high moral stature ? The kind of
world order that man is seeking is to be preceded by a
moral revolution. It is not a question of having a better
United Nations, it is a question of having a better moral
outlook, at both the individual and the national level.
There will always be good individuals but what is needed
is good nations. The ethics is the same—for individuals,
as for nations. Also, no activity can be divorced from
moral and spiritual perceptions. The spirit of renunciation
and service should inspire everybody, more specially the
leaders. The national leaders have to be world leaders.
They have to think of the interests of the world as a whole,
and not of the narrow interests of their own countries only.
In private or in public, they should be model men and
women in moral terms. Not just moral, but really great in
every way.

THE PANACEA

Education is often cited as the panacea of all the maladies to which man is subject, individually or collectively. But what kind of education is that? If it is indeed a panacea, why has not that been yet applied to give relief to man in his individual and collective sufferings? One is reminded in this connection of Buddha's attempt to discover a way that would end sufferings for all and for all time. He was so moved to see human suffering that he left home in search of the panacea which he thought existed and which could save man from the maladies that plagued him. Christ was another saviour who voluntarily suffered crucifixion to save man from his miseries. There have been other saviours who have made the same attempt at great cost to themselves, but with what results? Has man's misery ended? If not, why not?

Indeed, man's miseries still continue. The reason is that he has not heeded the lessons taught by those great teachers. Some people have argued that those lessons are not practicable; others may have tried to incorporate them into their lives but have done so perfunctorily, or have only pretended that they are living up to the ideals those lessons represent and have, on that ground, claimed and received undue privileges. In other words, they have exploited others. As a result, the teachings of the saviours either never filtered down to the masses, or if they did, they did in a diluted, even in a distorted, form. They, therefore, never produced the intended impact on the people at large. Because of his own folly and selfishness

man has let his misfortunes continue as if there was
nothing he could do about it. Isn't it a pity ?

But what have the Great Masters taught ? If anything,
they have taught selflessness. You cannot and should not
wish anything for yourself which others have not got. If
you happen to have something others do not have, try to
share it with others. If, instead, you try to be special in
order to enjoy privileges, you only invite unpleasant
consequences for all, for yourself most of all. Yet this is
precisely what man has always been doing. 'Each for
himself—this is the motto he has followed. Nothing can be
more irrational than this. Animals, even birds and insects,
unite to solve a common problem. Their collective sense is
a lesson man will do well to learn. This is not to say that
man is altogether devoid of the sense of unity; he surely
has it, else his present achievements would not have been
possible. But this unity is not consistent, it shows itself
only in certain circumstances. When, for instance, there is
a war. Naturally, that unity is only temporary and based on
artificial divisions of race and country. How wonderful it
would be if such divisions did not exist at all! Physically
there may be any number of divisions, but the heart should
ignore them. 'No one is a stranger to you'—a recent
Indian saint taught. But man, from his very childhood,
learns to love some and hate others. It is his selfishness
that prompts him to make this distinction. It is his
selfishness that makes him miserable.

But how can selfishness be eradicated ? Through
education rooted in the teachings of the Great Masters.
Education means training in character, that kind of
character which rejects all traces of selfishness. It can be
the panacea of all problems when man is rid of the feeling
of separateness from others.

BODHISATTVA

One justification religion has is that it makes, or is intended to make, a man large-hearted, feel for others, and help them as best he can. One of the Upanishads says that when the thunder rolls, it does so as if it is saying to all living beings to practise self-restraint, to extend a helping hand to others, and to be compassionate. This sums up the whole of religion, both in theory and practice. No prayer, no religious act is complete without charity. Islam lays down how much of your earning you have to spend on charity. Other religions eulogize charity as a cardinal virtue to be practised not merely by making monetary gifts, but also by rendering personal services, no matter in what form. No limit is fixed in this. In Hindu mythology there is even the example of a sage sacrificing his life in support of virtue. Every Hindu prayer ends with the word 'Peace' repeated thrice. The word here means wishing well of all, physically, morally, and spiritually. The Buddhist prayer is more explicit : 'May all people be happy; may none be in pain.' Hinduism attaches great importance to the spirit behind charity. Whenever you give anything to a person, give it with utmost humility and reverence to him; if you can't give it that way, you had better not give it at all. The quality of a charity is to be judged by the attitude of the giver as well as by his means. A man with limited means giving the same amount as another person with means twice as much, certainly deserves more praise. There must be an element of sacrifice in the giving. If you give at a pinch—that is good charity. The

Mahabharata tells of a starving family dying because it gave away its last grain of food to a guest. This kind of sacrifice places the charity on the highest level.

The story goes that Buddha offered his life to save the life of a small kid. A still greater sacrifice he made was when he deferred enjoying the full benefit of salvation to help other people get the same benefit. He now welcomed the suffering which he had once set out to overcome, for he did not want happiness for himself alone, he wanted it for all. So he kept wandering and preaching ceaselessly, denying himself the rest and comforts he needed. Buddha illustrates what religion ultimately boils down to—serving others even at the cost of one's own salvation, the highest achievement in life.

But which comes first, one's own salvation, or serving others? Buddha served others only after he had attained his salvation. Following his example, should not one first concentrate on attaining salvation, and after having reached that goal, then turn one's attention to the problems of others ? Can a blind man lead another man ? What is one going to teach when one is ignorant oneself ? This question led to an acrimonious debate, ending up in a split among Buddha's followers—one group concerning themselves with their own spiritual evolution (*Arhatship*) and another group giving a higher priority to service to others. The second group have the *Bodhisattva* aspect of Buddha as their ideal. A charge against religion is that it makes a man selfish. The *Bodhisattva* ideal gives the lie to it. No wonder it has such an appeal. But cannot a man try both—being an *Arhat* and a *Bodhisattva* at the same time? In such an attempt alone, anyway, does man's future lie.

FEMINISM

If feminism means giving women their due, the movement is welcome, but if, in the process, it breeds suspicion and distrust between men and women it had better be curbed. The seeds of discord can only widen the gulf, not bridge it. The problem cannot be solved by apportioning blame, it can only be solved by love—'the highest wisdom (is) to return no harm to them that harm you,' as *Tirukkural* says. The need is for men and women to live together on terms of the deepest love and goodwill. The spirit of selflessness should inform everything they do to each other. The question is not how much each can get from the other, it is rather how much each can give to the other. The joy is in the giving, giving cheerfully, unconditionally, spontaneously. This is possible where there is genuine love. Genuine love may have a weak start, but it grows and can keep growing. One has to have the will to love. 'Give and take', but giving comes first, and if there is giving, one *may* then expect to receive. Better not to expect, for one may not get what one expects. Conditional giving is always devoid of joy—as much for the giver as for the one who receives. Love for love's sake is the ideal. If one starts calculating how much love one has received in return, one will always find one has received much less than what one could reasonably expect. This is the beginning of the irritation which keeps growing, leading ultimately to a complete rupture. Perhaps you will be rude and hurt the other party, maybe inadvertently. If you do so, can you expect the other party to remain the same ? He or she is bound to resent.

What is the corrective ? The corrective is in the recognition that there can be no genuine friendship between two selfish persons. Both have to be ready to sacrifice. When both are demanding, clashes will follow and a rupture is inevitable. No permanent relationship is possible where both are trying to get the maximum, giving nothing if possible, or only the minimum, in return.

There is no doubt that women have suffered much indignity throughout history. Physical weakness has tempted men to take advantage of them in every possible way. They have been sold in the open market as animals. If this has stopped, they continue to be treated as slaves at home. Marriage only legalizes such treatment. There are well-meaning laws on the statute, but in practice they never give women the relief for which they were enacted. If today feminists tend to be impatient and demand more and more stringent measures in favour of women, they cannot be blamed.

But the question is if law is the answer to all the problems which women face. Experience has shown no. Law cannot compel men to give the love women need. The fact of the matter is that both men and women need each other's love. They are, in fact, complementary to each other.

In the Hindu tradition, God is sometimes man, sometimes woman, sometimes man and woman both at the same time. This is to emphasize that man and woman are basically one, one in spirit. If this oneness is recognized, the question of rights and privileges between them becomes irrelevant. The only logical relationship between them is one of love and respect. If husband hurts wife or vice versa, the result is, both are hurt.

RACISM

Racially or otherwise, no country today is entirely homogeneous. It is more of a mosaic of many races, each distinct with its religion, language, and culture. If there is a basic unity—there is one no doubt—-it is not easily discernible. Somehow or other, these races are together and they happen to pass as a nation. If they are bound together at all, their ties are chiefly geographical and political, which hardly mean anything. The word 'nation' today seems to have become rather vague and ambiguous. A nation, composed of diverse races, is naturally a weak fabric; it may break apart any moment under the slightest pressure, from within or without. Many nations are today in this unfortunate situation. This happens because many races have moved away from their original habitat and suffered elsewhere. They perhaps did this from greed or just because they had to. They shifted centuries ago, yet they retain some of their old features, linguistic, religious, and otherwise. Perhaps pride has inhibited any change.

Race, language, religion, and culture are supposed to unify, but they also divide. The division is sometimes vertical and, on that account, self-defeating. It's self-defeating because no race can stay totally isolated and yet prosper. 'Learn from others' should always be the motto for individuals and groups both. It is natural if racial groups are unlike each other in their thinking and tastes. But the differences are no index of superiority or inferiority, they are just by-products of history.

A society which welcomes a free influx of a wide spectrum of races receives more than gives. Each race that comes from outside brings with it much that is new; it brings new wisdom, new talents, new thoughts, all of which add to the intellectual and cultural wealth the society already possesses. A society which follows the policy of banning entry of new races is like a man who shuts himself in a room without ventilation. Its human resources, however rich they may otherwise be, soon begin to decline. This is the price a country pays for being isolationist.

But the races that go into the making of a nation will be wise to keep a low profile. If they are too ambitious they will make troubles for themselves as well as for others. Each of them has the right to retain its separate identity, but it has also to fit into the national model. It may have its own ambitions but surely it can have no ambitions that override national interests, or the interests of other races. If racism is nagging many nations today, it is because most races today have a feeling that they are being passed by. They blame not themselves but others for their own backwardness, if they are indeed backward. It often happens that some of the smaller races are more enterprising and, as a result, they dominate the economic scene. They are doing very well, still they are not happy. Perhaps they will complain that they are not given due political importance. Often the racial minorities have an exaggerated notion about their past and they dream some day they would regain their past importance. If that dream is not in the process of being fulfilled fast enough, they try to find a scapegoat and they may find that scapegoat in the Government.

Racism is nothing but a kind of exclusiveness which, beyond a certain point, may prove harmful as much to the nation as to the race concerned. Let each race prosper, but let it prosper only to help other races and the nation of which they are part and parcel. The ideal condition is where each racial unit is able to grow only to contribute to the growth of the nation as a whole. Let each stay distinct if it so wishes, but let it stay as an instrument in a symphony. That is to say, let it show its excellence, but only to produce a collective excellence of the highest order. In details, they may be separate, but, in their wholeness, they must be one.

SCHOLARSHIP

Wise men of India say that a scholar commands respect everywhere whereas a king commands respect only within his territory. What is the point they are trying to make by this? The point they are trying to make is that scholarship is superior to political power. Granted that that is what it is, the question arises: Wherein lies the superiority of scholarship? Also: What is scholarship?

Scholarship, in the ordinary sense, is the same as learning. You are a scholar if you have read many books and if you know many subjects. By virtue of your knowledge you are able to guide others when they are at a loss to decide what is the right thing for them to do. You become their natural leader. Even a king who is politically supreme may need your guidance. The power of birth, of wealth, or of the sword—all these are no doubt great, but greater is the power of the intellect. In fact, these powers become useless, even harmful, if not backed by the power of the intellect. Like the brain in the human body, he leads the whole mass of men and women, in his own society and even outside. This is where the superiority of scholarship comes in.

But suppose a scholar, despite his knowledge and intellectual eminence, is selfish, mean, and vicious, will he still command respect? People may dread him but surely never love and respect him. If he is bent on doing harm to others he can do much greater harm than anyone less intelligent, less scholarly. An intelligent crook with the additional advantage of scholarship can very well prove a menace to society. Scholarship commands respect when it is the scholarship of a good man. So it is the character of the man which makes scholarship important and not scholarship by itself. Yet scholarship is praised because it is the key to the treasures of the human mind, ancient or recent. An acquaintance with these treasures enriches, or is expected to enrich, you in more ways than one: It gives you a larger overview of things and also a clearer insight into them. If you utilize this knowledge in your own personal life, you become a better individual, not only intellectually but also morally and spiritually. 'To know is to be'—is the dictum of Indian scholarship. The knowledge of water does not quench the thirst, only its drinking does. Knowing of high principles is good, but applying them is better. Even a feeble beginning is laudable, for a child's first steps truly mark the beginning of a future marathon champion's race. Knowledge is a useless burden if not accompanied by wisdom. Knowledge is the means, wisdom is the end.

What is wisdom? Wisdom is character, the by-product of a man's evolution in moral and spiritual terms. Scholarship is supposed to help in this evolution; it is in fact the catalyst. A wise man may or may not have studied much, but has acquired a natural goodness which shields him from all that is evil. He will much rather hurt himself than hurt others. He is honest, frank, and straightforward; as if by instinct he knows what is right and will always stick to the right even at great personal sacrifice. Over the years he has practised the basic principles of moral goodness and has thereby laid a fine moral foundation on which he stands secure and firm against temptation. It is the beauty and fragrance which result from years of austerity and self-discipline and which surround the whole personality of the wise man. Only such a man can guide himself and guide others. Only such a man commands respect everywhere.

RELIGION WITHOUT DISCORD

Religion professes to be a way to moral and spiritual perfection. Prayer, fasting, charity, and pilgrimage are among the many ways and means religion prescribes for this purpose. Countless people, known or unknown, have adopted these methods over the centuries and still do the same though not all with the same results. Perfection is the aim but few, very few indeed attain it. People still keep trying, hoping they will some day be perfect. If you ask them, 'What is perfection?' they may not be able to give a clear, or even the same answer. Each individual has his own conception of perfection, and what is perfection to one may be no perfection to another. Paradoxically, a man, widely recognized as perfect, will most likely deny that he is perfect. The pursuit of perfection is perhaps the best test of a man who is perfect, or is, at any rate, on the way to it. Conversely, when a person stops pursuing perfection, convinced that he has already reached the goal, one may be sure that he is still far from it. Perfection shows itself not in the rigidity with which one practises religion, it shows itself in the kind of person one is. Is one honest, kind, generous, friendly, humble, selfless? These, among other qualities, are proof that one has reached the goal religion envisages, that is, perfection. Nevertheless, one will not want to admit that one is indeed perfect. A perfect man would like to see himself still better than what he is. There is no limit to what is called perfection.

If perfection is the goal of religion, why are there then many religions and why are then conflicts between one religion and another? More to the point, why do those conflicts lead to violence including bloodshed? A close study of the different religions will show there is much that is common among them. They all give priority to honesty, goodwill, friendship, and service. In short, the essence of all religions is the same. If there is a difference it is in details, say in modes of expression, in rituals and minor practices. This difference is natural, even necessary. Not all of us are alike. We have different tastes and temperaments. Religion should make room for these different tastes and temperaments. The goal remains the same—perfection; but the ways of reaching that goal differ. The ways may differ but they do not, need not, clash with each other.

Yet the paradox is that there are conflicts, often accompanied by violence. On scrutiny it will be found that conflicts arise not over any religious issue, but over loaves and fishes, that is, over material gain. One group wants to enjoy more political and social power over another, and it invokes religion to justify its claim. Or it may plead that it is being a victim of political and social discrimination because of its religion. The grievances may be flimsy, but they are inflated beyond all proportions. People, otherwise friendly and living like good neighbours, all of a sudden find themselves sharply divided. Often clashes do take place and blood spills. Neither side wants it to happen, it still happens.

It is an insult to religion if in its name a man hits another. What is needed is to get down to the heart of religion which is love. Those who are searching perfection have to behave as if they are already perfect. They can bear no ill will towards others, they can bear only love, if necessary even at great personal sacrifice. The question of hurting others never arises. Truly religious people may differ from each other, but can never be inimical to each other. They can only agree to disagree. They are the true salt of the earth.

THE WITNESS

There is someone in each of us who is watching all that is happening around us. Who is he so watching in us? He is no other than the person whom we refer to as 'I'. We say, 'I'm doing, I'm enjoying, I'm sorry, and so on.' Every time we say something we use this 'I'. This 'I' is common to us all. This sense of identity is present in every living being—man or animal. Indian philosophy claims even plants have this sense of identity. This may be debatable but it is now widely accepted that plants are also highly sensitive. This sense of 'I' is a common factor among us all. There is only one 'I', one common Self, which binds us all together. That is to say, we are really one.

But how are we one? We are separate from one another in every way; no two individuals are alike even within the same family. Take the case of men and women. Are not men different from women? Are not races and communities different from each other? The difference is not only physical, but all-round. Similarly, man is fundamentally different from animals. Animals are also different from each other even within the same species. Where is the oneness?

The oneness is in the being who is watching. The same being is watching, though he keeps varying his forms. One may wear a shirt one day, another day a coat, but the person remains the same. What he wears is not the person. The same is the case with his name. A person may have any number of names, but he remains the same man. There is the same being in man and animal, though he may assume innumerable names and forms. The names and forms are not the reality, the reality is the being. Since the being is one and the same in all, it has to be something unconditioned, unqualified, without any attributes, without beginning and without end, indescribable. The names and forms change, they can be seen and felt, but the being which is always the same cannot be seen or felt.

But if it is the same being in all, how is it that no two individuals are seen behaving in the same way? Again, they may be friendly with each other, or inimical. If it is the same being, why should they differ from each other, or bear ill will towards each other? Their differences are not just superficial, often deep-rooted. How can such differences occur?

The answer is ignorance. The being is one and the same, but because of different names and forms which are like masks superimposed on the being, it appears as if there are many beings, each separate from the other. But how do we know that there is a common being, or there is any being at all behind the names and forms? The answer is: When the body stops functioning, ignorant people think it is death. That is the end of the 'I'. Is 'I' then the body? But when we sleep, the body is at rest, yet we dream we are going places, and we have all kinds of experiences. How can we have these experiences when the body is at rest? So the experiencer cannot be the body. Is it the mind then? But when we have dreamless sleep, the mind also seems to be non-existent. Both body and mind being inactive, the condition is similar to death, but it is not really death, for we soon wake up and we resume life from where we left it off. As if we had put aside the body and the mind for a while. But who did this? It is the 'I' in us, the being who is always watching, the witness. It is the same witness who at death leaves the old body with all its embellishments and assumes another body at an appropriate time. The witness is never born, it never dies, it only changes its names and forms. This witness is the common being, the Self of all, men or animals.

'FOR THE GATE IS NARROW AND THE WAY IS HARD...'

If you say you want to be a good man and live your life according to sound moral principles, you let yourself in for hardship, sorrow, and suffering. First and foremost, you discover that while you were telling yourself what sort of life you would like to live and what would be your 'dos and don'ts', weaknesses start surfacing within yourself which you never thought existed. Your fight against yourself starts from that point onwards and it gets more and more bitter as the days pass by. The hurdles are more within than without, and these difficulties within are always formidable. In spite of your firm resolve to remain morally irreproachable, you find to save your face in a difficult situation you won't mind telling a lie. Where there is a possibility to earn an extra amount of money by adopting unfair means, you'll without the least compunction use those means, however grossly wrong they may be, judged by the standards you have set for yourself. Your conscience may prick you, but you try to find comfort from the fact that no one is going to find you out, or that you are not the only one who is doing this, everyone else in society is doing the same. The fact that most people are really corrupt, or, at any rate, you love to think they are, gives you a good excuse for doing what you know is wrong. There is also the possibility that by trying to be honest you earn the hostility of people among whom you live and work, for they themselves are dishonest and if you are not one of them, they will always be in dread of being betrayed by you. They will be happy if you join them in their immoral activities. If you do not, they

will create situations to compel you to do so, or otherwise
remove you from the scene, by hook or by crook. Maybe
you will for a while resist the temptation or threat they hold
out to you, but finally succumb to their pressure, arguing
there is nothing else you could do in the circumstances.
Indeed it takes much courage and strength of mind to stay
true to one's principles when hemmed in by such hostile
forces.

The common counsel given by wise men in such
circumstances is 'fight or flight'. That is to say, either you
fight to the last, paying any price necessary without
surrendering your principles, or run away from the company
of people who try to draw you away from the path you have
chosen for yourself. This is sound advice, but is it always
practicable? What is one to do if one has no choice but to
surrender or be crushed altogether? A truly moral person
will gladly accept death, but never compromise his
principles. Christ rightly says, the way is indeed very hard,
it is like going uphill. The path of evil is always easy, but
there are people who deliberately choose the difficult path
of moral perfection. They may slip now and then, but they
never lose heart, never stop struggling, either. They may fall
for the umpteenth time, but they are up on their feet each
time they fall and start fighting to reach the goal. It is this
fight that is to be respected. The ultimate success may never
come. A truly moral man, however, keeps hoping that he
will someday succeed. Success or failure, his eyes are
always fixed on his goal and he keeps pushing forward as
best he can.

It is such people who are described as 'the salt of the
earth'. It is such people who make life worthwhile and the
world livable. Such people may be few, but they always
constitute a power that hauls up the rest of their fellow-
beings towards a better and more moral life.

RELIGION AND ETHICS

It is difficult to imagine religion without ethics and ethics without religion. Religion and ethics invariably go together and sometimes they even overlap. A religious man has to be ethical just as an ethical man, whether he likes it or not, is also religious. Religion sanctions and supports ethics; ethics justify religion, for religion transforms a man completely, making him incapable of doing anything wrong.

But what is religion? How is it related to ethics? Why can't a man be moral without being religious, religious without being moral? Religion is a science of growth, growth towards perfection. If you are religious you will not be happy with what you are. You will say, 'I must be a better man, better in my human qualities. I will be better and better till I reach the level of a Buddha, or his like.' It may sound too ambitious, but it is better to have an ambition like this and keep struggling all the time rather than have no ambition at all. Religion gives a man the ambition and also shows him the way that ambition can be fulfilled. A religious man constantly feels the urge to struggle and grow better and better. He soon discovers that as he is practising religion he is acquiring, as if in spite of himself, more and more of self-control. For instance, he is less susceptible to temptations of money, power, fame, and sense pleasure. He tends to be austere, keeping away from things most people run after. He begins by telling himself what he should do and should not do, thus subjecting himself to a measure of self-discipline which becomes the foundation of his ethical life. He soon turns out to be a man who will not tell a lie, cheat others, use his power and position to exploit the weak, try to gain something to which he is not entitled, and so on; at the same time, he is kind, compassionate, and friendly to all.

Ethics and religion both can be individual and collective. Each individual has his own ethics and religion; so also each community. Ethics develop out of a consensus among the members of the community. Love and hatred are common to all living beings—man or animal. All animals love their young and hate those who they think are likely to be inimical to them. Most animals restrict their family ties to their children only; most of them also chase away their children when they are grown up enough to look after themselves. Some animals have their own herds in which young and old both live together. They have a loyalty to each other and also to one among them who is their leader. They have a code of conduct, devised by their elders for the safety of the individual members of the herd and for the safety of the herd itself. The primitive man follows the same principle. Gradually his sense of responsibility grows, covering not only his own family but also other families in the neighbourhood. If anybody is hurt, it is as if he himself is being hurt. It is out of this feeling of oneness that ethics grow. Love and consideration for others inhibit wrong doing between one another. Slowly a full code of what is done and is not done develops, holding together all organized units of mankind, from family to the entire civilized society.

Concurrent with ethics grows religion, one helping the other. Religion means being better and being better means being more ethical. The goal is the same as is the means. Religion and ethics converge on the man who has reached the goal, that is, the perfect man.

EDUCATION AND RELIGION

The debate will perhaps never end about mixing religion with education. Just as some people are convinced that education should be absolutely secular, there are people equally convinced that no education is complete unless it is based on religion. Those who object to religion argue that it is 'irrational', 'obscurantist', and makes people 'other-worldly'. It also creates a bias for which no real reason can be found. They further argue that this being an age of science and technology, education should be strictly in accordance with objective facts, it should not admit of any hearsay, or anything speculative. Religion, on the other hand, takes things for granted, an approach education would never accept. Education insists on precision, objectivity, and logic. It is the by-product of knowledge and reason. Knowledge is handed down from generation to generation, but it can be challenged and is challenged. The new generation may or may not accept it. Nothing is in fact sacrosanct. Knowledge grows because nothing is accepted as final, an attitude antithetical to religion. Religion again tends to look backward, and is to that extent a hurdle to progress.

All this is granted, but is there any basic difference between religion and education? If education aims to create better men and women, a better society, a better world, religion does exactly the same. Education helps man control nature so that it can be used to his benefit. Man is now much better off than he was centuries ago.

He has material prosperity such as he never imagined possible in the past. More perhaps is in the offing. Life has improved, but has man himself improved? Can education claim any improvement in terms of man's innate qualities, or in his relations with others? Why is there any war at all? How far does education contribute towards preventing it? Ironically, if anything, education makes the horrors of the war worse by discovering new weaponry. If education is intended to improve mankind as a whole, it has done nothing of the sort, man remains a savage even today; only he has become more sly, has acquired more powers to harm others, and is himself more unhappy than ever before. He has of course a larger array of pleasures at his disposal, thanks to his education and his inventive genius, but those pleasures are mere baubles, if not also debasing.

What about religion? It has the same purpose as education—turning out better men and women. We do not see why education and religion cannot work together. One may object to the methods religion employs—prayer, for instance. How can any sensible person pray to a God whose existence is in doubt, or who, judged by the way He runs the world, if of course He is the one running it, is a most erratic person? There are other objections, too. Whatever that may be, it must be admitted that it is among the much-maligned and much-misunderstood religious people that good men and women are found. If by praying to a non-existent and self-willed God, men and women turn out good, why should they not pray to Him?

If both education and religion have the same purpose why should both not be used to improve mankind?

FAITH

All religions stress the importance of faith, but what is faith? Faith is belief in God or some person that will always come to your rescue, should you ever be in trouble. The source is not very clear to you, but you are nonetheless certain that he will never let you down. Experience may sometimes prove otherwise, but you still continue to believe in him. If he does not come to your help, you console yourself saying that perhaps it is all for the best. Your belief may seem irrational and it may receive jolts again and again, yet your faith in God or that person remains unshaken.

Faith is in fact the sheet-anchor of religion. You have faith in somebody and you cling to him as your friend, philosopher and guide. He inspires you and shows you the way to follow to reach the goal you have in view. That 'somebody' may be an invisible person. It does not matter, for you are sure he exists, as if he exists for your sake. You feel his presence, you hear his voice prompting you what to do, and you feel safe being under his care. Sometimes you doubt if you will ever succeed, in reaching the goal, but he scolds you, coaxes you, and restores your self-confidence, and you resume your struggle. The faith in him sustains you whenever there is a hurdle to cross. You feel diffident, but he encourages you, and you soon discover spurts of fresh energy and strength within yourself.

What is important is faith in yourself. This faith comes when you believe someone superior to you is looking after you. If this person is visible and present with you, it is better; but even if you cannot see him but feel his presence, that may serve your purpose just as well. You feel you are safe so long as he is around. This faith makes all the difference between one individual and another. The man with faith is strong, determined, and always ready to struggle; the man without faith is shaky, cannot decide what to do, may take a step or two, but will soon begin to feel it is not worth the trouble, or it is not for him anyway.

But how long can you have faith in someone you have not seen? True, you may have doubts about his existence, or his willingness and ability to help you. But there are numerous people who testify that they have trusted that invisible person—God, or whoever else he may be—and found it worked. Why can't you at least try? You can try, and if you find there is no response from the person concerned, you can then turn to your own resources. You have to depend upon somebody—either yourself, or God or some superior being.

The fact of the matter is that there are hidden sources of strength in all of us. We are not aware of them and many of us do not even believe they exist. The faith makes us conscious of them. To begin with, we have faith in some outside agent. This leads to faith in ourselves by virtue of our connections with that external agent. We say, 'So and so is my guardian and protector, so why should I worry?' If this goes on for a while, we begin to feel we are part of that agent and eventually, we even feel that we are that agent himself.

The real strength is not outside, it is within. Religion helps us discover this fact. Not only strength, but knowledge, everything. For our real being, our Self, is everything we look for, inside or outside. Faith is faith in this Self, in the infinite capacity of our Self.

THE SENTINEL

They stand as sentinels—the mango tree and the *bel* tree at the two extremities of Belur Math. As if they are guarding the legacy of the godlike men who lived here not too long ago. It has to be saved for mankind's sake. The trees are witness to the rise and growth of the Ramakrishna Order, lovingly called by a scholar 'The Ramakrishna Empire'. Here, like the seers of old, Swami Vivekananda preached the loftiest thoughts known to man. Together with his brother-disciples, he raised a band of young men who would love truth and worship man as God. They would spearhead a world-wide movement to forge unity among mankind through love, goodwill, and friendship.

Swami Vivekananda was bursting with energy. He behaved like one possessed. Sometimes he would sit under the mango tree, sometimes under the *bel*. He was always talking, always inspiring people. He would now quote from the scriptures in support of what he was saying, next he would point to his Master Sri Ramakrishna as an illustration. He was a man in a hurry, for he knew his end was coming near. He was impatient, sometimes he was angry. He came down heavily on those who were slow, or not enthusiastic. 'Give whatever you have to give, empty yourself, and be blessed,' he would urge.

Here the trees saw Swami Vivekananda and his brother-disciples in their highest spiritual moods. If you go near fire, you feel its heat. Those who came in contact with them immediately recognized that Ramakrishna was working through them. To be with them was like being with the Master. It was an experience in itself. The whole atmosphere in the monastery was surcharged with spirituality. You felt it as soon as you stepped on the ground of the monastery. You would ask yourself, 'Is it real, or am I dreaming?' You would come again and again. You would tell your friends about the place. They would come too, and in their turn, ask others to come. This is how the message spread far and wide. Religion is to be lived. People came and saw how it could be lived. It was something the world was waiting for.

And then fell the blow—Swami Vivekananda suddenly passed away. Some people thought the Order would collapse. Nothing of the sort happened. Swami Brahmananda took over as leader, Sri Ramakrishna had already named him as the future leader. Taking the hint Swami Vivekananda passed on his authority to him. Swami Brahmananda led by example. He himself was always in a meditative mood and he wanted the monks to spend most of their time meditating. Thus he strengthened the spiritual base of the Order. 'You can serve others if you are truly spiritual'—this was the burden of his message. By following his advice, the Order is growing from strength to strength.

Monks of the Order, however, believe that it is Mother Sarada Devi's blessings that help the Order grow. They feel it individually and collectively. The trees witnessed how Mother once came to bless the monastery and how it received her. The monastery was decorated under Swami Brahmananda's personal supervision. When Mother arrived, he stood at the head of the monks with folded hands. The monks chanted appropriate hymns. It was as if Mother Durga was coming. Mother blessed the Order. Miracles keep happening as a result.

Are not the trees lucky to witness all this?

TO FULFIL AND NOT TO DESTROY

As quoted by Matthew, Christ is supposed to have said, 'I am not come to destroy, but to fulfil.' Much was wanting in man and society before Christ. There was needless cruelty on common people by those in power. Society was splintered into small, warring groups. Temples swarmed with crooks of all sorts. There were good people, but they were few in number and they were helpless. They hoped, as they had been told, a saviour would come soon, but, meanwhile, their misfortunes were piling up. At last, Christ came. People recognized who he was and they were full of hope. But he was spared only a few years in which to give man any real relief. He had barely started when he was picked up and crucified on suspicion that he was conspiring to overthrow the ruling authority. Yet the thoughts he had planted in the minds of a close group inspired them to strive for sanity among people and help create a better world despite persecution. The movement Christ started still goes on. It is not organized, not visible even, yet individuals hear Christ's call 'Come to me' and they rush to respond.

Christ's predecessor, Buddha, also, declared that his mission was to fulfil and not to destroy. Both knew it was easy to destroy, but that solved no problem. What you destroy leaves its root and it soon appears again, maybe in a more virulent form. If you fulfil, you add what it lacks. Buddha and Christ were not social reformers. They filled in the gaps which had left society weak and vulnerable. They gave thoughts and ideas for man to follow; they did not promise a comfortable life, they rather promised hardship and suffering. They said no price was too high for a good life and character. Be perfect—this was their message. To understand what is perfection you have to have a model. These teachers provide that model.

Buddha was born into a society where scholars wasted time talking about academic matters, hardly ever paying any attention to improving their personal character. Religion and morality were much talked about, but seldom practised. Appearance was more important than reality. There were more hypocrites than honest and sincere people. The masses were confused, also exploited. There was no one to inspire, no one to show the way. At this crucial moment Buddha appeared, filling in the gap. His life was his message. He did not argue, he demonstrated. He showed how self-help was the best help, how strength was to come from within, not from without. He was more concerned with individuals than with society, like his successor Christ was. Each individual had to plough a lonely furrow. He reduced philosophy and religion to principles of daily application, to the practice of some basic virtues. The focus was always on being. He was a man of the people and for the people. He taught in the language of the people and what he taught was simple, clear, and practical. He had a tremendous charisma and if he so wished, he could have led a social and political revolution. He did nothing of the sort. He lived his life. And he wanted people to be entirely on their own. 'Be a lamp unto yourself'—that was his final message.

Thus he fulfilled when people depended on what others had said.

THE STILL SMALL VOICE

Is there such a voice as the title says? Whose voice is that? What is its function? Why is the voice so described : 'still' and 'small' ?

The voice is God's—God speaking to Elijah on Mount Horeb. What did the voice say? It demanded the slaughter of all enemies of God. Elijah was willing, in fact, eager, to carry out the command. The voice was only testing. It meant no carnage, it meant only surrender to God as it turned out later. 'Go, and return to me'—that was the final command.

So, the still small voice always asks us to return to God. We stray away from Him, He calls us back to Him like the mother bird does when she finds her chicks moving too far away from her protective wings. She seems to say at first, 'Will you please kill all my enemies?' The chicks, in a chorus, say, 'Yes, of course we'll.' They move as if they will carry the battle into the stronghold of the enemy. They start moving away from their mother, in search of the enemy. The mother bird watches, amused. The little ones dare further and further. The still small voice of mother warns, but the chicks pay no heed. Before any damage can happen, mother rushes, and with some blows of her wings, draws them back into a safer zone. Does God do the same with man? Does He want us to fight His enemies? Who are they? Are they inside man or outside?

There are, indeed, many enemies of God and they are both inside and outside of man. Ignorance is the source of these enemies. It is powerful, with myriads of its offshoots. God created man to fight ignorance, He wanted man to be His ally. Alas! he surrendered to it. God is since then calling man back to Himself in His still small voice. Does man hear it? He does, but seldom obeys. The consequence is—he suffers. The voice may be 'still', and 'small', but it is pressing, even commanding. Man, however, pretends he does not hear it; he ignores it as if it does not exist.

Throughout history this conflict continues—the conflict between the still small voice and man's ignorance. There is never a moment when the voice is silent or wrong. Is it God's voice? Yes, if you believe, but if you don't, let us say it's your own voice, the voice of your better self. Suppose you're bent on doing something, and the voice within warns, 'Don't do it, it's bad; if you do it you'll get into trouble.' You can't figure out whose voice it is. Does it matter? What matters is what the voice says. What it says is right, though you don't want to admit it. You admit it later when you suffer, when it is too late. Again and again, this happens, yet you ignore the warning the voice gives you. Why is it so? It's because of your ignorance, ignorance which is the root of your vanity and the attitude that you know better. The suffering continues so long as ignorance lasts. All the time the still small voice keeps speaking. It is like the mother bird always concerned for her chicks. Finally, your suffering reaches its peak and your good sense prevails. You begin to obey the voice. As you do so, the enemy retreats, your ignorance troubles you less. The voice is now clearer and louder. Like the chicks returning to their mother, you are returning to God, you are safe on the path the still small voice points to you. The enemy—ignorance—retreats.

RESIST NOT EVIL

Is it sound advice that we should not resist evil? If we do not resist evil, it will keep growing and will soon tear apart the social fabric. Crime will increase and life and property will be insecure. Those who are strong will do whatever they please and the weak will be left at their mercy. The law of the jungle will prevail. The evil propensities in man will grow unchecked and man will be reduced to a brute. Truth, justice, equality, friendship—all these will disappear, society will crumble, and civilization will be erased.

How do you keep crime under check if you do not resist evil? One well-known recipe which saints and seers advocate is—love. They usually say, 'Hate the evil, but love the evil-doer.' It is a good idea, but does love go so far as to totally eradicate evil from the human mind? Holy men and women have always preached love and have themselves loved others also, but it cannot be said that they have succeeded in changing human nature. This is no argument against love as a corrective force; nothing can rouse in man his good propensities more than love. When the good propensities are strong the evil propensities automatically lose their force. Somehow or other the evil that is in the heart of man has to be overcome. This is as much in his own interest as in the interest of the community. An evil man can never be happy. When he hurts others he hurts himself also, perhaps more so. The best discipline is self-discipline. You have to impose on yourself rules about how you are going to behave in different situations. There may be provocations, what will

you do then? Christ asks you not to react. If somebody hits
you on one cheek, invite him to hit you on the other—that
is his advice. Will you do that? Should you do that? Why
should you do that? Is that not cowardice? Whom you are
helping in doing that? Not him, any way. You are rather
encouraging him to behave in the same way with others.
You are not teaching him self-control, you are teaching
him irresponsible behaviour, for which he may have to pay
dearly someday. What does Sri Krishna say to Arjuna?
Just the opposite of what Christ advises. He accuses
Arjuna of cowardice because he does not want to fight
with his cousins over his rights. Arjuna says he will rather
live by begging than try to wrest from his cousins what
rightfully belongs to him by causing bloodshed. According
to Sri Krishna, this is not only cowardice, this is also
dishonesty. Arjuna does not and cannot mean what he
says. There is hate in his heart, but he pretends he is full of
love, an attitude for which no condemnation is too strong.
By all means, Arjuna has to be honest with himself. 'Be
honest and get killed, if the worst must happen', that is Sri
Krishna's advice.

Sri Krishna then goes on to expound when and where
good and evil overlap. They are basically one and the same,
but if you see them different, that is because of your own
ignorance, because both good and evil are within you. So
long as there is evil within you, you will see evil outside
and it should be your duty, as a responsible member of
society, to check that evil. Tagore condemns the man who
sees evil, but does not stop it. If you see somebody doing
something evil and you do nothing to stop him, you are as
much guilty as the man who does the evil.

Only people like Buddha and Christ who are free from
evil themselves can be excused for not resisting evil.

WITH CHARITY FOR ALL

Abraham Lincoln was a man who could rightly claim that he did not preach what he himself did not or could not practise. There is nothing on record to suggest he refused to show his natural charitable disposition in the case of one who was not in agreement with him, or was hostile to him. He, in fact, wished well of everybody, known or unknown, friend or foe. This was not merely a principle with him, this was part of his nature, a characteristic. A really charitable person is charitable always, in all circumstances, and to all men and women.

What is it that makes a man extend charity to everybody, irrespective of country or creed, irrespective of everything? 'Friendship and goodwill for everybody, never mind who he or she is, or what sort of person he or she is'—this is an ideal one can live up to only when one has the conviction that there is a basic unity underlying all the differences that characterize mankind. Not only that, one has to have also the feeling that man is basically good. If man is sometimes bad, it is often because of his circumstances. He is bad in spite of himself, circumstances forcing him to do a thing he does not like. And if he is bad, it is not that he is always bad; it is a temporary lapse and he can certainly avoid repetition of such lapses with a little determination and effort. You must have this kind of optimistic view about every individual, otherwise you cannot be charitable to him. Unless you have some love and respect for the person you are helping, your charity is no charity, it is a mockery, it is an insult. Above all, you have to have the feeling that in helping others you are in fact helping yourself. In extending your hand of friendship, you are bringing others closer to yourself, you are as if becoming one with them. In the ultimate, nobody is an isolated person. We are all together, interrelated, we are a single entity. A great man is great not because of his scholarship, political power, or wealth; he is great if he has a great heart, if he is able to love everybody equally. A great man, as Hinduism visualizes, is *samadarshi*, sees all, good and bad, big and small, as the same. Only a *samadarshi* can be charitable to all to the same extent. Everyone has his own idea of charity. With most people, charity means helping people of the same community, the same country, at the most. This is no charity, this is selfishness on a larger scale; this only intensifies exclusiveness, making the barriers that divide mankind stronger. A charity which divides is dangerous; if your charity is for your community only, you indirectly create rivalry between that community and other communities in the same society, help that community to acquire power to hurt other communities, less fortunate. In other words, you sow seeds of discord in national life. Real charity is charity for all, making no discrimination based on country, language, or creed. A truly charitable man is everybody's friend and well-wisher.

Industrial civilization has brought in its wake material prosperity for some nations. Other nations are still below the poverty line, or barely above it. This discrepancy is causing tension, even conflicts, among the nations. When a large segment of the human population is unhappy, can the prosperous nations merely look on? Can't charity be practised on the international plane? It is true that it is sometimes practised, but, more often than not, it is niggardly, and worse, strings are attached to it. That is to say, it is selfish charity, which is no charity at all. Where there is love and goodwill, there is no room for selfishness.

THE MESSENGER AND THE MESSAGE

' I have a truth to teach, I, the child of God,' said Swami Vivekananda. Prior to this, Sri Ramakrishna had solemnly declared that Swami Vivekananda was going to be a world teacher. Swami Vivekananda always resented such predictions about himself: he, for one, saw no basis for them, and he knew how people would ridicule him later when those predictions would prove wrong as they were bound to. As such predictions often came from a doting Ramakrishna he hardly ever attached any importance to them; still, because he felt embarrassed by such irresponsible remarks, he could not help protesting, as he did in the present instance with all the vehemence he was capable of. This only provoked Ramakrishna to assert with greater vehemence that what he had said would happen. And, truly enough, it did, as later days proved.

Ramakrishna took special care in training Vivekananda for the role he wanted him to play. It was not an easy task, for Vivekananda had a mind of his own and he was the last person to accept anything which, in his judgement, was not right. But it was neither Ramakrishna's way to impose anything on anybody, much less on Vivekananda who was his *alter ego* in more ways than one. All Ramakrishna tried to do was to help awaken the great powers lying dormant within Vivekananda. He knew once those powers awoke, they would burst the slender dam which now held them at bay and would overflood the world, remind man of his destiny, of the ultimate goal for which he must ceaselessly strive. He had infinite potential within himself and all he needed was to fulfil it, which he could only if he had faith in himself. If there had been a Buddha in the past, there could be more Buddhas in the future. This message of hope, courage, and self-help man was long waiting for, a message that India had for centuries cherished as a closely guarded secret and which Ramakrishna had lately unfolded. Vivekananda had at first rejected the message as a blasphemy, but the Master made him see the truth of it through experience and he had no choice but to accept it. The impact of this message can be seen in his own declaration, quoted earlier.

Meanwhile, preparations had been under way at Chicago for a Parliament of Religions where every religion was to send its delegate to present its viewpoint on religious issues. Vivekananda's youthful admirers of South India wanted him to represent Hinduism at this Parliament. He declined. What followed still remains unexplained. He changed his mind and he began to feel the Parliament of Religions was being held for his sake. Later, he even declared, 'I have a message to the West as Buddha had a message to the East.'

His very first words at the Parliament on 11 September, 1893, spelled out what that message was. He addressed the audience as 'Sisters and Brothers', a novelty which, together with his majestic bearing, thrilled the audience. The one theme on which he constantly harped in the course of the speeches he made, at the Parliament and outside, in the following years was: The unity of mankind and man's divinity. In a suffocating atmosphere of racial pride and prejudice, and self-debasing religious dogmas, the message was a welcome relief. Just as the message inspired people, so also the messenger, by his life and character.

SUCCESS AND FAILURE

Success and failure are said to be two sides of the same coin. That is to say, they are one and the same, but viewed from different standpoints they appear different. If two countries are at war, the same result is victory to one and defeat to another. The viewpoint changes the nomenclature.

Does it mean then that the one who wins the war and the one who loses it are the same? Not exactly. They are different but only temporarily. They may some day interchange their positions and whoever was earlier declared to have won the war may turn out to have only lost it, if judged by the loss the country has suffered, in life and property. When this happens victory becomes a mockery; the other side may come to regard defeat as a blessing in disguise. If nothing else happens, the jolt it suffers may mark the beginning of a period of hard thinking and hard work, leading to unprecedented prosperity in its history. The nations involved in the Second World War, including both winners and losers, are a case in point.

Perhaps this is why the *Gita* asks us to regard success and failure, victory and defeat, as the same. To explain: It means that we are not to attach too much importance to either success or failure, victory or defeat. Why? Because what seems success at first sight may very well prove failure on close scrutiny. The *Gita*, pragmatic and wise, cautions against too hasty a reaction. We all have to go a long way and there are bound to be many ups and downs. The first success is not the last just as the first failure is

not the last. To be practical, we had better take everything
with equal indifference, bearing in mind that the end is yet
to come. There is no room for euphoria if there is success,
there is also no reason for us to give way to depression if
we fail. We may fail again and again, yet we must go on
trying. Life means trying. Not to try is death. Again to
quote the *Gita*, 'Your duty is to try, no matter what is the
consequence.' We should keep trying till we reach the
goal. 'Not to be content with the small things we have
before us, but to try to achieve what is the best and highest
though it may be far away'—this is what the Upanishads
preach as being the goal of life. To be content with the
first taste of success is suicidal, it is like preferring to
remain ignorant when full knowledge is open to us.
Discontent is the seed of growth. We may be content with
everything, but we should never be content with ourselves.
A man who has achieved much has every reason to be
content, but if we ask him if he is content, he will
promptly say he is not. He will say all he has achieved is
nothing, he is still far from the goal he wants to realize. To
such a man, the goal always keeps receding from him. In
fact, no one knows for certain if there is such a thing as
'the' goal. What seems to be the goal turns out to be a
mere watershed.

Success is not a single event; similarly failure. Both
are compounds of many events, in fact, many successes
and failures. Both the words, success and failure, are
misnomers. There is no success which is not a failure,
there is no failure which is not a success; the perspective
determines both and the perspective changes. What is
important is the content and the content is the same for
both viewpoints.

RENUNCIATION

Religion talks of things man should try to realize and also of things he should try to avoid. The problem is, man has a natural tendency to do just the opposite: to leave alone the things he is asked to try and get, and to run after what he is told to shun. He is thus always in a dilemma between what he should do and should not do. If he is able to follow strictly what religion says, then he has no dilemma and he is on safe ground. But is it possible? Is it possible for everybody? Few, very few indeed can avoid the dilemma and know for certain what they have to do and do the same too. For most people, the path is difficult. It is like 'the sharp razor's edge', as the *Katha Upanishad* says.

The difficulty arises from man's weakness for sense-pleasure. Sense-pleasure is ephemeral; everybody knows it, yet man finds it difficult to resist its temptation. He fights for it, regardless of the price he may have to pay for it. He may finally get it only to lose it after a while, or discover that it is not what he thought it was. The things that attract man most are: money, health, beauty, good reputation, and power. He may already have a good measure of each of these, yet he is not satisfied and wants more and more. He keeps grumbling all the time, as if he deserved more but did not get it. He is possessed with the desire to get sense-pleasures; he would not mind using unfair means to get them. He finally ends up making a mess of his life. Religion cautions us against being carried away by temptation. The real test of character is in being able to resist temptation. If you cannot resist temptation,

you commit errors for which you may have to pay dearly
in terms of physical and mental suffering.

Just as man errs, he can also rectify his errors. Happily
for him, he can judge what is right and what is wrong and
he can also avoid what is wrong if he has a strong mind.
So, in the final analysis, strength is the secret of success in
man's struggle against temptation. Religion does say what
man should do and should not do in different situations,
but it is up to him whether he will follow those
prescriptions or not. Religion is very clear and categorical
on the subject, but if man still misbehaves, it is because
the path is difficult and man is weak. It takes much
strength of mind and hard practice to be able to resist
temptation.

But it is a mistake to think that renunciation is
something negative. Renunciation is opting for higher and
better things in place of vulgar, degrading, and distasteful
things. There are two sources of enjoyment open to you:
one, purely sensual and gross; another, intellectual and
refined. Some people derive their greatest pleasure from
food, clothing, and the power they can exercise over others;
others are happy if they have good books to read and good
friends with whom they can discuss moral and intellectual
issues. It is not that they are looking for some personal
benefits from such discussions; they are concerned about
human misery and they want to devise ways and means to
end that misery. It was exactly because of this reason that
Buddha opted for the life of hardship in place of a life of
pleasure and comfort to which he was born.

Renunciation is not poverty, but refusal to be caught
up in the web of inferior pleasures. It is a question of
priorities: to a man of renunciation the highest priority is
the joy of acquiring moral refinement at any cost.

RELIGION : USES AND ABUSES

Religion is supposed to improve a man morally and spiritually. He is expected to be kind, honest, and just. These qualities are his hallmark. If he is found wanting in these qualities, people will begin to wonder if he is truly religious. The test is not in his religious practices, it is in his character. But how many people will prove truly religious, judged by this criterion? Few, indeed very few.

The popular idea about a religious man is that he prays, visits holy places, obeys laws laid down in the scriptures and as interpreted by the priests. This is enough to prove that he is religious. What sort of man he is nobody wants to know. Society holds him in high respect. He behaves as if he is close to God and this respect is his due. He then starts telling people what they should do or should not do. He soon has a following of his own and he begins to think he is responsible for their well-being. He holds himself responsible not only for their moral and spiritual well-being, but also for their secular well-being. He begins to interfere in everything concerning his followers. He holds himself up as a model for others to follow and he behaves as if he is God's representative on earth. He demands unquestioning obedience from others and he gets it too. Inevitably this turns his head. He is not satisfied with the power he already enjoys, he now wants more power. He will be glad if he can make his presence felt by everybody in the country. His popularity with his followers gives him leverage for this. He claims he is their sole guardian and he has to protect them from aggression by others. Often he complains that he and his people are not able to practise their religion the way they like because of interference by other groups. Other groups, however, say that the truth is just the other way round. Thus, society is divided into groups along religious lines and these groups continually fight among themselves. But who lead them? It is the so-called religious leaders. They are 'religious' leaders all right, but are they truly religious? Do they exhibit any of those qualities which religion is supposed to produce? They are mostly fanatical people, who use religion as a means to satisfying their worldly ambitions. They are arrogant, selfish, and worldly-minded people. Religion is only a mask with them. How much blood they have spilled in the name of religion! Is religion responsible for this, or man's greed?

True religion makes people think more of others than of themselves. They are also strict about the means they adopt to achieve their ends. They will not compromise on Truth. They try to raise the moral level of their daily life. Whatever they do by way of religion is only to improve their character. Some people are good right from their birth, but they can be better. Religion gives them the impetus to grow better and also shows the way. They may be involved in politics, or may be doing something for the good of their people, yet they never deviate from their principles. A religious man is a religious man in all situations. To him his first priority is his religion which requires that he should always be honest, kind, and just. Prayer and other religious practices do help, but they are not the criterion by which they should be judged. What kind of people they are is the only criterion. If under the garb of being religious, people fight others over worldly gains, whether for themselves or for their community, they are abusing religion.

SERVICE TO MAN IS SERVICE TO GOD

Since God is everywhere, He must be in man also. The Bible says, 'God created man in His own image.' That is to say, if God has a form, it must be a human form. Whatever form He may have, God is certainly most manifest in man. Man is, in fact, closest to God, since he is by far the best among all living beings. He is intelligent, he can discriminate, he has creative powers, and he can also think for himself. He may or may not be close to God, he is certainly God's favourite, else why would God bestow so many gifts on him? Again, man alone can morally and spiritually so develop as to be only second to God. Man is the only testimony to what God is like. He is truly an image of God. This is why serving man is like serving God.

All religions preach the virtue of charity. No Hindu worship is complete without charity. And whatever you give as charity must be of the highest quality. How can you give to God something you would not like for yourself? Whatever you give must be good and you must also give it with great love. The *Taittiriya Upanishad* (I.II.3) says, 'When you give something to somebody, give it with due respect; if you cannot give it with respect, you had better not give anything at all.' We should remember even a needy person has his self-respect. Just as what you give is important, the way you give it is also important. If you give somebody something with contempt, or even with reluctance, you hurt the self-respect of the man, which is worse than not helping him at all. He is unhappy that he has to accept your help. He may say, 'Thank you,'

but does he mean it? Doubtful. Charity, so given, does not
help either party—the giver or the person who receives the
help. We should deem it a privilege if we are able to serve
anybody. We should be grateful to him for accepting our
service; we should not expect him to be grateful to us. If
we serve with respect and humility, that will make all the
difference. If we serve merely because we are moved by
the poverty and suffering of an individual, there is the risk
that our manner of help will carry a sense of superiority
and arrogance. If this happens, service will no longer be
service, at least, it will not be service to God. It will defeat
the very purpose of service.

But what is the purpose of service? The purpose of
service is to help us feel the presence of God, wait on
Him, and to have an intimate communion with Him. It is
as good as prayer. It is in fact more than prayer, for when
you pray there is always a barrier between you and God.
At least you do not see Him, you cannot talk to Him, you
do not even know if your prayers are being heard by God.
When you serve a man as God, you can see how he is
responding, whether he is pleased with you or not. If you
are able to serve him well, nothing is more satisfying to
you than that. A smile on his face is your best reward. The
more you are able to serve, the more you feel blessed.
There is much suffering in the world. It is God who is
suffering. How can you look on when God, your Lord and
Master, is suffering? You rush and help as much as you
can. Maybe you cannot do much, but what of that ? You
are happy if you are able to do your best. Help with
anything you can. Prayer is good, but prayer is only
words. This is better because this is prayer in action. So
service to man is service to God and it is the best way to
serve God.

PARADOXES IN EDUCATION

When you find widespread corruption among educated men you begin to wonder, 'What is education and what is it for?' Is it merely some knowledge? But knowledge of what? Suppose there is a scholarly person who has studied extensively but is morally vulnerable, would you say he is educated? What purpose has education served in his case besides enabling him to strut in society as someone very important? But is such a man really important? In what sense is he important? He may be important to himself, but is he important to society? If he is not honest, such a person can be very mischievous, and a mischievous person is more a liability than an asset to society. Suppose there is another man not as learned but honest. Whom would you prefer? A good and healthy society is one where the majority of people are not only educated, but also honest and ready to help one another. If, on the other hand, they are educated but not honest and have no feeling for others, would society be happy and progressive?

Education defeats itself if it does not make a man a 'better' man. But 'better' in what sense? Better in every sense of the term, but, first and foremost, as a human being. Knowledge is said to be power, and the first thing an educated man has to acquire is knowledge: knowledge of the world he lives in and his duties and obligations to it. He has every right to think of his own well-being, but education makes him conscious that he cannot live in isolation, he is part of the society he belongs to, and he is as responsible for the well-being of his society as he is for his own well-being. If a man is selfish in spite of his education, his education serves no purpose and he is a sham. If, in addition to being selfish, he is unscrupulous, beware of him—he can be a menace to society.

It so happens that there are many such people in society today: people who have this so-called education and who are also selfish and unscrupulous. To make matters worse, such people may be in high positions in society, with power to do whatever they please. They can start an ethnic riot, even an international war, for selfish reasons: for instance, to secure their political hold on the country, or to divert public attention from their own misdeeds. Each move they make is so camouflaged that their real motive is never known. Ironically, such people may later figure in history as international heroes. It is not that their shortcomings are never known, but they are overlooked because of their position and the influence they have over the media. Facts may also be twisted for this purpose. How much misery they inflict on people, in their own country or outside! But they get away with it. And they are all 'educated' people!

Education is not merely knowledge, it is how that knowledge is used. It is character based on universally accepted ethics. These ethics are: honesty, fairness, and love of all beings. No one without these qualities can be called educated.

But where are these qualities to come from? Are they to drop from the blue? No, each individual has to try and try over the years to acquire them. It is easy to be a scholar, but difficult to be morally good and sound. It takes much strength, courage, and sacrifice.

Education is all-round development. The process goes on continually. The consummation is in the character you finally develop. The criterion is in your moral perfection.

THE MASTER AND HIS DISCIPLE

Sri Ramakrishna was generally soft and kind while dealing with his disciples, but, if necessary, he could be very stern too. For instance, in matters of food, specially its quantity, he could be uncompromising. He would not like anyone to have a big meal at night. Night is not for sleep, it is for meditation, according to Sri Ramakrishna. He would tell everybody the quantity of food he could eat at night. If he exceeded that limit, he would be annoyed. Similarly he would not permit anybody to tell the smallest lie in fun. A lie is a lie. You start with a small lie, and soon you find yourself telling the biggest lie, keeping the face straight. With Sri Ramakrishna, Truth was God, and God was Truth.

He, however, believed in giving positive, rather than negative, thoughts to his disciples. There were hardly any 'don'ts' in his teachings. He would talk about the ideal and explain again and again how to reach it. Up to a point, what he taught was the same for all; but after that, variations followed. Some are exceptionally gifted: you cannot satisfy them with what you give to the average. You have to give something special to them. The ideal in their case must be more difficult, to match their potential. The best in them must be forced out. Surely big race horses cannot be treated at par with aged coach horses.

The most promising, yet the most difficult disciple Sri Ramakrishna had to deal with was Swami Vivekananda. He was one who would not accept anything just because it came from a holy man or a holy book. He was out to debunk everybody and everything. Yet he was a genuine seeker. He had been hearing religious lectures and had also met a few religious leaders. He was not impressed. Finally, he met Sri Ramakrishna. He was not impressed, but he felt here was somebody entirely different from the common run of so-called holy men. He was not educated, but he was intelligent, and sincere. He was crazy perhaps, but he had strong common sense. He felt baffled about Sri Ramakrishna, yet he felt drawn towards him. As regards Sri Ramakrishna, he literally, to the point of being ridiculous, doted over him.

What is interesting is the way Sri Ramakrishna taught him. He never made it seem that he was teaching Swami Vivekananda. Normally, whenever a discussion started, Sri Ramakrishna would lead it, and everybody else would listen. Swami Vivekananda seldom agreed with him, and sometimes he even pooh-poohed what he said. He once said he liked Swami Vivekananda because he argued. He was obviously referring to his ability to think for himself. Anyone without a mind of his own cannot make any progress even materially, let alone spiritually. Sri Ramakrishna believed that each individual was unique. If he was not independent intellectually, he would be misled, even exploited, by others.

Swami Vivekananda was at first opposed to the Vedantic idea that everything, in its essence, was divine. Sri Ramakrishna did not argue with him. He handed him a book and asked him to read it out to him. It was a book on Vedanta. Swami Vivekananda said what the book said was all nonsense. Sri Ramakrishna said, 'Never mind what it says. Just read it out to me.' Slowly the idea sunk into Swami Vivekananda's mind, and it was backed by experience also. Vedanta later became the main plank of what he preached to the world. He saw God everywhere and in everything.

THE RAZOR'S EDGE

If you choose to follow an ideal, you cannot afford to be happy-go-lucky: you have always to be watchful about what you are doing. Every step you take should be directed to the goal you have in view. You are like a ship heading for a particular port through a narrow channel with sunken rocks on both sides of it. You have to steer very carefully, or else you may founder on one of those rocks. If the ideal is high, the steps leading to it are invariably steep and narrow. You climb with great caution, or else you may slip. Anything you want to achieve—in religion, literature, politics, or sports—you have to deserve by hard work.

The ideal is not the same for all. It varies from individual to individual. Some people are content with their physical well-being. If they have money enough to enjoy life, they are happy. Others want intellectual pleasure. Another class of people, not too many in number, want spiritual satisfaction. Among such people there may be a few, maybe a handful only, whose first priority is spiritual enlightenment. They are ready to give up everything, but they cannot and will not give up spiritual enlightenment.

But what is spiritual enlightenment? It is difficult to define; only when you have it do you know what it is like. You then know for certain that you have attained something unique, something that gives you the feeling that you have everything you wanted. Those who have any kind of spiritual experience often use words which convey no meaning whatsoever to common people. They talk of light within, they hear voices, they are always full of joy, though there is no apparent reason for their joy. Surprisingly, mystics in all ages and countries have used more or less the same terms in describing their experiences. But of course it is not important what kind of language they use; what is important is the kind of people they are. They may not be rich, or learned, or politically important, they are just humble people, likely to pass unnoticed; yet they are remarkable people in many ways. For instance, they enjoy peace and happiness within themselves, an experience not given to many; also they radiate the same peace and happiness wherever they are. They expect no reward from any quarter, not even a word of appreciation for whatever they are. They may even be misunderstood, but they do not mind. If you happen to praise them, they will protest, saying you are mistaken. Nothing external seems to attract them. The source of their joy and happiness is within themselves, though what it is they themselves do not know, much less others. It is not that these people are life-negating; they accept life with all its joys and sorrows, but they seem to be above everything. They are always unperturbed. Not only that, they treat all people as friends. They can never hurt anybody; they can only love. There are not many such people, there are only a few, but they are everywhere, in every society.

What do we have to do to be like such people? Self-annihilation is the key to the attainment of the kind of character such people have. We have to wipe out all traces of selfishness and install in its place love and compassion for our fellow-beings.

This is not easy. It is like walking over 'the razor's edge'.

LOYALTY

Loyalty is love which never wavers, which is always steady, unquestioning, deep, total. It is also one-sided, not based on any expectation; it is its own reward, love for its own sake.

True religion is this kind of loyalty to God, whether as a person or as an idea. A truly religious man never for a moment doubts that God exists. He is there always with him, sometimes within, sometimes without, watching over him, helping him, guiding him, at the root of his being, the source of his inspiration, not separate from him; at one level, God and he are one and the same.

If God is a person, He is clear, well-defined, with a form, the form the devotee likes best, handsome, ever benign, love personified. Sometimes the devotee merges into Him, sometimes God merges into the devotee; they become one. As if God deliberately becomes human, with all the faults and frailties of the devotee, so that they can be closer to each other, enjoy each other's company, have fun together, laugh, and play. Everyday they devise new games, devise new ways of teasing each other; sometimes they lose sight of each other, but the separation, even if for a moment, is unbearable, and soon they are again together, love redoubled. This is how the play goes on, interminably.

Religion is love of God, whether as a person, or as an idea. Either way this love works miracles. It changes the devotee into what he thinks God is. If he thinks God is purity, he becomes pure himself; if God is goodness, he becomes good himself. A man changes according to the company he keeps. Being in the company of God all the time, he acquires the qualities he attributes to God. This being in the company of God is what is called religion. God may be an imaginary being, but the change takes place all the same. This is because to a devotee God is real. He is as real as he himself; if possible, more. Even if God is only an idea, that idea is concrete to the devotee. That idea possesses him, changing him completely. He is that idea personified. It is his loyalty that triggers the change.

Given loyalty, creeds and dogmas become redundant. Rituals may be totally dispensed with, or retained only to the extent that they express the love the devotee has for God. Love has its own rules, its own modes of expression. It is sovereign, not bound by any conventions, any dictates from any authority except his own heart. A devotee may not get anything in return from God, but he does not mind. He is happy if he is able to give himself up to God unreservedly, unconditionally. Love is totally selfless, it is its own *raison d'etre*. All religions talk of love as being the sure way of winning God's grace. In fact, God Himself is love. If we love God, we love Love. In loving Him we fill ourselves with love and our whole being is transformed with the beauty and the grandeur which emanate from love. If there is such a thing as divinity, love is that divinity. Loyalty to God is both the means and the end of that love.

But how can we be loyal to someone we know nothing about? Unless we know for certain that there is a being called God and He really lives and cares for us, how can we trust Him? Love is said to be blind. It is that blind love which we have to have in dealing with God. We do not know each other, yet we trust each other as if we have known ourselves since the beginning of time. Loyalty heeds no reasoning, it is irresistible.

THE GURU

There is much confusion about the word guru. Some people think it is a mischievous word, for it makes the common man think that he can get whatever he wants, on earth or in heaven, through the guru. But who is this guru? Whoever he may be, people who believe in the guru cult have the impression that he is second only to God.

The idea may be repugnant to many, but the guru cult is common to all religions, though not in the same manner or form. When the bishop, the imam, or the brahmin priest in the village says something, that is the word of God. Few will dare go against it. What he says may sound illogical, even harmful, yet educated people will accept it. Whoever questions it will bring social opprobrium on himself, if not more serious consequences. If the guru is a crook and also has a large following, he is capable of doing great harm to society. Nevertheless, he is obeyed.

The idea of a guru is not necessarily wrong. Anybody wanting to learn something has to have a teacher. Whatever may be the field of his study, a competent teacher at hand is a great help. Without a teacher, he is a blind man groping in the dark. But woe to him if his teacher is himself blind! It is still worse if the teacher is a cheat. He will exploit him. But some day or other he will be found out. Because many so-called gurus eventually turn out to be fake, the very word guru has a bad reputation.

But are all gurus bad? There are gurus who themselves hate the word guru. They are humble people without any pretensions to being superior to others. They may not even want to teach others though they are competent. If pressed, they will say they know nothing.

The word guru has a special connotation to a spiritual aspirant. He is as good as God Himself. The aspirant knows that without his guru's help he cannot make any progress in his spiritual struggle. He is entirely dependent upon him. The spiritual path is so difficult that without a good guru, the disciple will never reach his goal. A good guru deems it his responsibility to lead the disciple by the hand. If the disciple fails, he blames himself; if he succeeds, he is as happy as if he himself had succeeded.

In the Hindu tradition, a qualified guru is one who knows the way to the goal and has himself reached it. Such a guru may not want to teach, because the task is not easy. First, he has to understand the disciple and his requirements; then, he has to guide him along the path best suited for him. He has to be with him constantly to make sure that he does not falter. Sometimes the disciple will lose heart and the guru has to keep his spirit up. Sometimes he may lose his faith in the guru himself and may turn to some other guru. In that case, the guru merely waits in patience, or tries in all possible ways to bring him back to the right path. The disciple may make mistakes again and again, but the guru never deserts him. He only feels sorry.

What does the guru hope to get by doing all he does for the disciple? Nothing. Often the disciple is completely ignorant of what the guru is doing for him. In fact, the guru does not let him know what he is doing. He does not expect a word of thanks from the disciple. He is like a lamp giving light but wanting nothing in return.

THE DISCIPLE

It is not easy to be a good disciple. He has to be intelligent, hard-working, and have complete faith in his teacher. The teacher may be rude, scold him at the slightest mistake, and sometimes may even be indifferent. The disciple has to have the kind of loyalty that an old pet dog has: The master may more often kick him than feed him, but he does not mind. He sticks around, giving the master whatever service he can give. The disciple is exactly like this dog. He knows the guru has much to give, but if he does not give it to him, he only blames himself, feeling that he does not deserve it. He, however, waits in patience, hoping that the guru will some day grant him his wishes. Meanwhile all he does is serve his master as best he can. He need not even tell his master what he wants. The master knows best what he needs. Let the matter rest with the master. If the disciple says what he wants, maybe he will make a gross blunder, asking for what is not at all good for him. Let the master decide what he should have and when. To be a good disciple is no doubt difficult.

But suppose the master is not a good man at all. Suppose he is selfish, crooked, even wicked. A disciple has to be careful while choosing his guru. If he chooses a wrong guru, he will suffer all his life. But how can a disciple be sure that he has chosen the right guru? Suppose he hears his friends speak of a certain individual as being a good guru. They tell him wonderful things about him: how he reads the thoughts of others, how he

cures diseases, how he can see things happening miles
away, and so on. To most people, the proof of a good
guru is in his ability to perform miracles. It may also be
in the eccentricities of his food, clothing, and life-style.
He must be out of the ordinary in order to impress the
disciple. From mere hearsay he feels he is the man he is
looking for, and when he meets him, he has no doubt that
his guru is right before him. Indeed, it is difficult, if not
impossible, for an ordinary man to decide who is a real
guru. A real guru is the last man to let others know how
good and great he is. He would prefer to pass as a very
ordinary man. Only another man, equally good, can
recognize him. Only a guru can recognize another guru.
A disciple may test his guru but may only make a fool of
himself. Yet he should test his guru at that risk, if only to
realize the futility of judging him by any known
yardstick.

According to the Indian tradition, each disciple is
his own guru in the final analysis. If he is a good
disciple, he finds that the guru is within himself, not
outside. The guru is his own mind; the mind refined by
the discipline he has gone through over the years, either
at his guru's instance, or on his own. If he has a
problem, his own mind will provide the answer. The
guru may not be accessible, but the answer will carry
the guru's authority. The disciple will never miss his
guru; he will always feel his presence within himself.
The guru's power is not physical, it is spiritual. That
power is lying dormant in the disciple; the guru's task is
to awaken that power. How he awakens it is not a
mystery; he awakens it through the efforts of the
disciple.

'GO FORWARD'

Here is a cryptic message of Sri Ramakrishna with an import much deeper than one would suspect. By this message you are being asked not to be satisfied with where you are, but to go further. But go where? 'Go and see for yourself'—that is the answer. Buddha pointed his disciples to the stairs of a building and said, 'Here is the way to the roof.' The disciples asked, 'What is there on the roof?' 'Go and see for yourselves,' Buddha replied. Why did not Buddha tell the disciples what was there on the roof? Obviously, because they would not have understood. Suppose Buddha had said, '*Nirvana*,' the disciples would have then shot at him a hundred questions to get a clear picture of *nirvana* and if Buddha had obliged them by answering each of their questions, would that have satisfied them? 'The taste of the pudding is in the eating,' the saying goes. One must eat the pudding oneself to know what it tastes like. Any amount of explaining would not serve any purpose. One has to have a direct and personal experience to know what a thing or place is like, no account of it, however true and vivid, can convey the same feeling as one has through one's direct and personal experience.

'Go forward' is a motto for everyone, no matter who you are and where you are. Being content is a virtue in certain conditions, but it is a weakness if it means that you are satisfied with whatever you are—foolish, ignorant, or morally weak. It is a virtue if it means that you are satisfied with your material conditions because you are more concerned about your moral development. Where the choice is between moral perfection and material prosperity, you opt for the former. For instance, if you are poor because you will not compromise your moral principles and you do not mind being poor, you undoubtedly deserve to be complimented. But if you are satisfied because you are lazy or incompetent, you should be condemned.

What is life for, if not for progress? To improve, to be better in every respect—that is the goal of life. Even if you want to progress materially, there is no harm in that provided that progress does not hamper your progress towards moral perfection. A king can also be a saint; in fact, that is the ideal. But what is moral perfection? Let us say no one knows for certain. Each individual has his own concept of moral perfection. It is also possible that the same individual defines moral perfection differently at different stages of his growth. This is natural. What you think is right as a child does not seem right to you when you are an adult. We ought to have the courage to reject whatever seems to have outlived its utility. The story of human civilization is the story of many such rejections. When a civilization gets caught in a rut, it is doomed. The same applies to individuals.

Life is like a river. If it does not flow, it stagnates and finally dies. Similarly a man must always go forward. If he does not, he is dead, though not physically, but intellectually and morally. If he goes forward, he may discover new worlds, within himself and without. What he discovers within himself is more important: within the depths of his being lie new visions, feelings and emotions, unfathomable in their richness. 'To know is to be,' goes the dictum. Out of that discovery he emerges a new person in the fullness of his perfection.

11 SEPTEMBER 1893

This date stands out as a landmark in the history of East-West relations, for it was on this date that the best minds of the two hemispheres met on the same platform for the first time. The occasion was an inter-religious dialogue bearing the pompous name, The Parliament of Religions. In reality, more pomp surrounded the event than the name would suggest.

The Parliament was Charles Bonney's brainchild. Bonney, an eminent lawyer commanding respect from all sections of people, was a highly imaginative person. The Parliament was held at the Art Institute, a newly constructed building meant for art exhibitions. It was a large, gray, limestone structure in the style of the Italian Renaissance. Four (some accounts say, seven) thousand people, comprising representative intellects of the day, both secular and clerical, anxiously waited for the Parliament to begin. There was a hush like inside a church. At the stroke of ten, the delegates arrived, headed by Cardinal Gibbons and President Bonney. The delegate who at once caught the eye was a young Hindu monk, Swami Vivekananda, conspicuous for his 'gorgeous red apparel, his bronze face surmounted with a turban of yellow'.

Speeches began: first, the organizers welcomed the delegates and the latter then responded. Swami Vivekananda was several times invited to speak, but he declined, for, as he himself says, 'My heart was fluttering, and my tongue nearly dried up.' Late in the afternoon, the Chairman insisted that he speak right away. Swamiji had now no option left: he rose to speak. One account says, '...his face glowed like fire.' Did some Power take possession of his body? Was somebody else speaking through him? The question arises because he used to say later, 'I am a voice without a form.' More significant, he addressed the audience as 'Sisters and Brothers of America'. A most unconventional way of addressing an audience. Who prompted him to use these words? As if all barriers had been removed and humanity as a whole had become a fraternity. As regards the response of the audience, reports say, 'Hundreds rose to their feet with shouts of applause. The Parliament had gone mad; everyone was cheering, cheering, cheering!'

When quiet returned, Swamiji made a short speech. What did he say? The burden of his speech was India's age-old idea of 'Unity in Diversity': the idea his Master had practised and preached. He quoted two beautiful verses. One was about rivers rising from different sources and ultimately becoming one in the sea. In the same way, he said, different religions shed all their differences when they reached God. Another was Krishna's assurance that people might choose any path they liked, but they eventually would come to him. In other words, religions were like paths leading to the same goal.

To most people this was an objectionable proposition. How could all religions lead to the same goal? Yet it was this that made Swami Vivekananda the most popular figure in the Parliament. People wanted to hear him again and again. Why? Because his thoughts, they felt, were 'as broad as the heavens'. They saw he was preaching no sectarian religion; he was preaching Truth, the common goal of all religions. He, therefore, pleaded for peace and goodwill between one religious community and another.

A hundred years have passed since Swami Vivekananda uttered those words. The world, still torn by religious dissensions, needs those words as much as when they first fell from his lips.

LET US DISAGREE

No two persons are alike in thought, speech, and action. Why should they be? Each individual is unique. He thinks, feels, and acts in his own way. He is himself, not a copy of somebody else. If he is not himself, he is worthless.

We need variety. Cowper says, 'Variety is the very sauce of life.' He might as well have said variety is the very 'source' of life. Only dead things have no variety; living things are distinct, separate from one another. Variety makes them what they are.

Man shows his variety most in his thinking. Just as no two individuals think alike, no individual thinks the same way always. His ideas change as the years go by. He thinks, reasons, learns from experience; change in his thinking is inevitable. If he does not change, he is a dead piece of wood.

Man is superior to other animals because of his mind. Similarly, one individual is superior to another because of his mind. Those who are superior lead the rest of mankind. They give new thoughts and ideas which shape the course of human history. They inspire, enlighten, and help create better individuals. Such people are not the monopoly of a particular country or age. They are the common heritage of man. Often those thoughts and ideas are impersonal. They pass from one mind to another, like electric waves, across time and space. No one knows for certain when and where they first originated.

Those thoughts and ideas may be lofty, but it is man's prerogative to question their validity. He never accepts things on faith. He questions, examines, and verifies. Unless he is satisfied from the results he obtains, he does not accept.

It is easy to agree with what others say, but difficult to disagree. It is difficult because you have to have your reasons for disagreeing. It is more difficult when you have to disagree with a powerful majority. And they may be people who have vested interests and by giving out your views freely, you are perhaps hurting them. They are not likely to forgive you. You may even risk your life by saying what you honestly think and feel. History is replete with such instances.

A happy and progressive society encourages free enquiry, free thinking, and free expression of thoughts. There is no question of any kind of regimentation. Naturally there is much disagreement, much debate, much searching for truth. We may err, but we want to have the right to err. We do not want to be told what is right or wrong. We want to discover it ourselves.

This is not to say that we have nothing to learn from others. We certainly have much to learn from others and we will always go on learning, but we will also think, question, and argue. We will not accept anything unless we are convinced that it is right. What we need is the courage to disagree. Let us disagree, but disagree only where there are reasons to disagree. Let us not impose our views upon others, for we can never be sure that our views are correct. What we think correct today may turn out totally wrong tomorrow. What is Truth ? We do not know. But we can nevertheless search for it. To be able to search for Truth is important, but more important is to be able to admit our failure to realize it. We may never know the truth, but let us not stop searching for it. Let us all the time keep arguing, sometimes agreeing and sometimes disagreeing with others. We will gladly agree if we feel there are reasons to agree, but we will also have the courage to disagree where our judgement says we should disagree.

'LET THE LION OF VEDANTA ROAR'

The above is a quotation from a letter Swami Vivekananda wrote to his friends in Madras from the USA. The friends had congratulated him on his good work and in reply he wrote the letter. What did he mean by this quaint expression? What he next says is still more quaint! 'The foxes will fly to their holes.' Obviously he is using some metaphors, but what has he in his mind? In what sense is Vedanta a 'lion'? And what does he mean by 'foxes'?

The religious situation in India very much disturbed Swami Vivekananda. Religion had come to mean caste. If you observed the caste rules, then you were religious. And what sort of caste rules? The most absurd, irrational, and heinous. It is your birth that determined your caste, no matter what sort of individual you were. A shudra's son was automatically a shudra, similarly a brahmin's son was automatically a brahmin, regardless of his character. Caste was originally a very sensible social arrangement, based on an individual's character and aptitude. All people are not alike, different people have different temperaments and aptitudes. The same vocation cannot suit everybody. Caste accommodates everybody, giving each a place where he or she can feel comfortable and can also give to society the best he or she can. Caste, according to Swami Vivekananda, has nothing to do with religion as such, but it can help religion if it is observed in the spirit in which it was conceived. It was intended to help each individual develop his or her talents; instead, caste, as it was practised then, served to hinder growth in many cases. The

worst feature of caste is to treat some people as
untouchable. It is admitted that you cannot freely mix with
everybody at the physical level; hygienically it is not
desirable. But if you have to keep away from anybody, it is
not because of his caste, but because of his unclean body.

What pained Swami Vivekananda most was the
condition of the masses. They were not only shudras by
caste, they were also poor, illiterate—and exploited by the
rich and the brahmins alike. They did not even receive the
solace religion could offer, for they were not allowed to
enter temples and participate in religious practices. There
was nothing they could expect from man or God.

True, India was a land of religion, but where were the
religious men and women? Swamiji found, next to caste,
most people were concerned with rituals only. Love of
God is the heart of religion. This was conspicuous by its
absence in the life and character of the so-called religious
people of the day. There were scholars who spent more
time discussing religious issues than being religious. The
whole scenario disgusted Swamiji. He was more interested
in the character of the people than in their beliefs and
practices. He felt only Vedanta, which preached the
divinity of men and women, could save India. First and
foremost, people must understand the purpose of life. The
purpose of life is to raise your moral and spiritual
standards till you reach the level of the godhead. Vedanta
says this is possible. Men and women have again and
again demonstrated this. Nothing short of it can satisfy
you.

Here is a message which gives you hope, courage, and
strength. Many things pass as religion which make you
feel you are worthless. You are only a 'fox'. Vedanta, on
the other hand, makes you feel you are a 'lion'.

THE VIVEKANANDA ROCK

The Vivekananda Rock is so called because Swami Vivekananda once spent some time there in meditation. This was before he left for the USA to attend the World's Parliament of Religions in Chicago in the year 1893. He had been travelling around the country for nearly three years, sometimes on foot and sometimes by rail, and he had now come to the southernmost tip of India in Cape Comorin. Constant travel had exhausted him physically. He was also mentally disturbed by the conditions he had seen in rural India. He saw poverty, ignorance, and tyranny of caste wherever he went. The lower castes were treated like 'next door to brutes', to quote Swami Vivekananda. The rich and the educated were selfish. They had no feeling for the common people. This is why Swamiji said, 'India's national sin is the neglect of the masses.'

The overall picture of India was indeed depressing. Swamiji felt there were three problems which must be tackled immediately: uplift of the masses, giving women the same status as men, and eradication of the caste virus. He wanted educated people to take the lead in these matters. But they were only for themselves. They did not think they had any obligation to help the poor and the backward. Swamiji blamed the prevailing system of education. It made people selfish, mean, and wicked. Earning money was the only purpose of education! They learnt to be smart and clever, but they never became true men.

Swamiji had lived with people of all classes during his travels, from princes to peasants. He studied India from close quarters. Just as her degradation pained him, he was struck to see that religion was everybody's first concern in India. Even the humblest man thought his salvation more important than material progress. His daily life was governed by some simple moral principles, honesty being foremost among them. He loved God and also loved his fellow men, irrespective of their differences from him. Swamiji saw real greatness amidst poverty, ignorance, and social injustice. Swamiji felt this incredible feature in Indian character was the outcome of centuries of a life dedicated to God. He wanted this saved by all means.

What worried him was the poverty of the people. 'There can be no religion on an empty stomach,' his Master used to say. How long could a starving India have faith in God? He wanted western affluence added to India's rich spiritual heritage. He could not bear to see India's masses starving. His Master had taught him to see God in man. Here is 'God' suffering from hunger. But what could he do ?

With this tormenting thought in his mind, Swami Vivekananda arrived in Cape Comorin in the last week of December 1892. There he noticed a rock far into the sea and it must have been a strange whim which made him decide to go and meditate there. While meditating he had an *experience* which made him feel that his Master wanted him to go to the West. For a long time, his admirers in Madras had been pressing him to go to the USA to attend the Parliament of Religions scheduled to be held in Chicago in September 1893. He had so long deferred his decision, but now he was convinced that he should go. His friends were happy and helped to make his voyage possible.

Swami Vivekananda's visit to the USA marks the beginning of India's national awakening. To this historic event, the rock, with the monument since built on it, bears witness.

WHAT MAN CAN MAKE OF MAN

If there is too much violence today, let us regret it, but not assume that it is inevitable. Violence is not natural, it is unnatural. And because it is unnatural it can be checked, even eliminated. It is possible to have a society where violence is more an exception than the rule. If there is a provocation, a cultured man may either ignore it, or may never express what he feels. He may merely smile and put to shame the person who provoked him.

Man has come a long way since the time he followed the rule 'Eye for eye, tooth for tooth'. He now knows it is better to forgive. If he forgives, he wins. He is judged not by his physical strength, but by the largeness of his heart. Others may wrong him, but he will keep quiet. If he does not retaliate, it is not because of weakness, it is because of his conviction that man is essentially one and by hurting others he hurts himself. In the larger interests of humanity he would much rather have himself hurt than hurt others. He may be put down as a coward, but he will not mind. To him the welfare of his fellow men is his first priority. He wants to live for others.

Only man can think in terms of mankind as a whole. Not only that, there are individuals whose concern includes even animals, insects, and vegetables. They feel one with everybody and everything. To them the world is one single unit. It is like a human body where one diseased cell can paralyse the whole system. Swami Vivekananda truly said that even a single atom could drag the whole universe behind it!

The fact has to be admitted that we all are one and we

must think and act accordingly. This is true pragmatism. We cannot continue to think in terms of races and countries as we have so long been doing; we may stay separate geographically, politically, even economically, but behind all such divisions there should be the feeling that we are one and we are interdependent. If there is trouble in any part of the world, the whole world is likely to be affected. Spiritual leaders may be aware of this, but the political leaders have to grasp this and frame their policies accordingly.

What man has done of man so far does no credit to him. It is an irony that man knows what he ought to do, but he does not do it. The fact of the matter is that power lies with people who do not know how to use it. Their views are blinkered. The immediate is most important to them, not what is beyond. They are blind to their own future. It is easy to follow the beaten track; the time has come when man has to try the more hazardous path of looking beyond the boundaries of one's own country, of using power for the good of all, of thinking of the oneness of mankind as a whole. Man owes much to himself which he can no longer shirk.

A national leader has to have an international outlook. He cannot say he is responsible for his own country only, he has to be responsible for the whole world. He cannot lead his country without taking into account what is happening elsewhere. He has to have a sound philosophy of life which will inform everything he thinks and does. Even his hardest political decisions will be rooted in that philosophy. Above all, he should be a God-fearing man. Only a God-fearing man is humble, selfless, a friend of all. The world needs honest politicians, whose means are as good as their ends.

'GOD THE WICKED'

This is an astonishing phrase used by Swami Vivekananda. In the same strain he has also said, 'God the poor', 'God the ignorant'. Not only he, even his Master, Sri Ramakrishna, has said similar things. Is all this not blasphemy?

There is a whole philosophy behind such expressions. According to this philosophy, man is essentially divine. He is divine, but his divinity is hidden. It is like the full moon sometimes seen fragmented, the original moon is always full, though it is not always so seen. Sometimes it is not seen at all. Whether the moon is seen at all or not, and however distorted it may be seen sometimes, it always remains what it really is—the full moon.

This simile aptly describes man's real nature and how it is seen distorted. Wickedness is not his real nature, it is only a distortion. This distortion can be corrected and when it is corrected, man shows his divinity. He is then a Godlike man, a wonder to everybody.

What are this man's specific qualities? First and foremost, he is honest. No temptation and no threat can make him tell a lie. He is selfless. He lives as if he lives for others. He never hurts anybody; he does not hurt an animal, or even a plant. He is above the barriers of race and country. The whole world is his home. Everybody is his brother or sister. If anybody, or any living thing is in pain, he is in pain too. If others are happy, he is also happy. He is one with everybody and everything.

Man is by nature selfish. How can he be so transformed that he will be like the kind of man described above? Has anybody ever seen such a man in flesh? Of course there have been such men and women again and again in history. Maybe there have been many more than we know of. They have come and gone, few people outside the circle of their closest friends knowing anything about their greatness. This was because their natural modesty made them shun publicity as far as possible. Even now may be found such people among the humblest in the world with divinity manifest in them in varying degrees, but if they are not known, it is because they prefer to remain unnoticed.

But if there is divinity in everybody, how is it that there is also wickedness in man? How can good and evil coexist? It is because man is ignorant of the truth that he is divine. If he were conscious of his divinity, he would have been consistently good, not sometimes good and sometimes bad, as at present. Each individual has to discover the divinity that lies hidden within himself under the mass of good and evil tendencies on the surface. It is like discovering gold under the earth. One has to dig deeper and deeper till the 'Gold' is found. But how does one know that there is any divinity at all within oneself? At first, one has a doubt about it, but when one sees people outstanding in their goodness, one cannot help but ask why one should not try and be like them.

No man is absolutely bad. Even the worst scoundrel is sometimes exceptionally good. It is wrong to permanently condemn anybody as wicked. If there is a blasphemy, this is it. Give him an opportunity to improve. With good education, encouragement and sympathy, even a hard-core criminal can improve. Instances of such transformation are many. This is possible because man is basically divine.

RELIGION AND POLITICS

The question is if religion and politics can go together. If a ballot is taken on this, an overwhelming majority will say 'No'. If asked why, they will point to what is currently happening in India, in the Middle East, and elsewhere. Not only now, in the past also, how much blood has been spilled just because politicians used religion as a tool to fulfil their political ambitions, or the so-called religious leaders adopted political means in order to increase their hold on the masses. Both the groups needed the support of the masses to achieve their respective secular ends. If necessary, they might even work together, though they bear nothing in common. As to the means, anything that works is acceptable to them. It is unfortunate that even religious leaders behave in that way. No wonder people blame religion for the conflicts that sometimes erupt between two religious groups.

But are the conflicts over any religious issue? Often the issue is entirely secular though it may have a religious coating. For instance, the issue may be whether or not a religious procession of one community can pass before a place of worship belonging to another community. It may cause some annoyance, but is it serious enough to justify violence? And what is the issue? The issue is to what extent a community can stretch its rights and privileges; there is nothing pertaining to religion as such.

Religion means self-restraint, humility, love and compassion for others. It means self-sacrifice. It abhors violence. No religion brooks the idea of jeopardizing somebody else's rights. A truly religious man cannot hurt others, he would much rather be hurt himself.

By this token, few religious leaders are truly religious. They are only masquerading as being religious, but they are mostly ordinary men and women using religion as a means of satisfying their worldly ambitions. They are after power. They mislead people, saying that their interests are at stake and only they can save them. They pose to be their guardians, but they are really seeking to consolidate their own position. What they are doing is in total contradiction of what religion stands for.

But is religion responsible for this? If people are dogmatic, it is not the fault of the dogma, it is the fault of the people who use the dogma to further their personal interests. This sort of misuse of a belief may happen even in politics. Two groups of people committed to the same political ideology may fight each other in a bid to increase their following. First, the difference is at the academic level, but soon bitterness grows and then violent clashes follow. The story is the same as in the case of religious differences. Just as the political ideology is not at fault, religion also is not at fault if people misuse it.

But a truly religious man keeps away from such squabbles. 'Live and let live' is his policy. If he takes to politics, he continues to be the same man: tolerant, humble, and honest. A political man without religion can be ruthless. He will invariably be selfish, vain, and corrupt. He will have no compunctions about what he does. Somehow or other he wants to prosper. His conscience is dead.

Religion is for all, more for those exposed to temptations. Pity the country where political people disavow religion, and religious people use religion to further their political interests.

COMMUNAL HARMONY

Many countries today are being rocked by communal strife. India happens to be one of them. It is strange that India, long known to be a peace-loving country, should now witness one section of her people fighting another. Stranger still is that the dividing line between these two sections is based on religion.

But are they fighting over any religious issue? No, so far as the facts are known. No religious belief or practice is at issue. It is not that one section has challenged the propriety of a particular religious belief or practice of the other section. In such a case, an academic debate would settle the issue; there would be no need for violence. If there is violence, it is because the dispute is over some material gain, or political and social rights. Because the issue concerns the interests of a particular religious group, it is treated as if it is a religious issue, which of course it is not. Because it is given a religious colour, it assumes an importance out of all proportions, and then, both sides get locked in a senseless fratricidal battle involving loss of life and property. The wounds they inflict on each other take a long time to heal. It is difficult for them to revive the good-neighbourly relations that previously existed between them. This is an irreparable damage. They cannot trust each other any more. Worse, they will start looking at every problem from the angle of their community as a separate entity, not from the angle of their nation as a whole. They develop a separatist outlook much to the detriment of the nation. So long as their own sectional interests are not in jeopardy, they are quiet and happy; what happens to the nation is of no concern to them. They want their separate identity safe and intact. This sort of parochial attitude naturally annoys the rest of the nation. This makes other people doubt if they are at all loyal to the nation. If there is a threat of a foreign aggression to the country, the police may start keeping a special watch over this group. This happens because the role of religion is misunderstood. Religion should make people broad-minded; instead, it sometimes makes them clannish.

People blame religion, saying that it encourages separatist tendencies. This is wrong. Religion asks people to treat others as brothers and sisters. It stands for truth and goodwill towards all. To a genuine holy man, all men are his friends, irrespective of race, religion, and country.

It is wrong to divide people in any country on the basis of religion or language. Just as a group of people may be identified by their religion, they may be identified by their language also. There is nothing wrong in that if they are so identified, but this should not imply that they need special measures for the protection of their language. In an ideal situation, the State need not protect them, other people will do that.

This applies more in the case of religion. Every individual has his own idea of religion and he should be able to practise it unless he infringes on the rights of others. There can be no dispute between one individual and another over religion. 'Live and let live' is the simple formula that should govern relations between different communities in the practice of their religions. A minority group may remain distinct and yet be part of the whole. The harmony rests on mutual love and goodwill.

31 MAY 1893

On the captioned day, Swami Vivekananda sailed from Bombay for America, one of the many passengers on board the ship Peninsular. How many had come to see him off? Not even half a dozen, as far as we know. Only two persons are mentioned in his biographies: Jagmohan, the Dewan of Khetri, and Alasinga Perumal, a school teacher who had come all the way from Madras. If he felt nervous about this voyage—he perhaps did, seeing that he did not know what awaited him at the end of it—the presence of these two friends must have acted as a moral booster. At one point, as he was getting ready to leave, he had felt that he had a 'message for the West'. He even said to a brother-disciple that the Chicago Parliament was being held for his sake. Judged against the difficulties he faced on arrival, the claim he had made would seem absurd. But what happened eventually amply justifies the claim. But let us follow his trail after his ship left Bombay.

Nothing is on record about what his fellow-passengers thought about him. Surely his yellow robe made them curious to know who he was. What they finally got to know is a matter of conjecture. Swamiji was not a man who would not allow people to come too close to him. He was a warm-hearted person. He must have talked to many people about things of common interest. What exactly he said is not of course known. What he said to Jamsetji Tata, perhaps the most distinguished of his fellow-passengers from Japan onwards, is known. Tata was then only a tradesman and he was going to Japan to buy match boxes.

He would bring them into India and sell them at a higher price. Swamiji decried this. He told him to turn to industry. He could make more money that way and also serve the country better. But he said, first and foremost, he should set up a centre of scientific research to discover new technologies for application to industry. Tata followed his advice with the results the world knows.

Swamiji travelled overland through parts of China and Japan, catching the *Empress of India* at Yokohama. He finally landed at Vancouver on Tuesday, July 25. His plan was to board *Atlantic Express* of the Canadian Pacific Railway immediately, but the train had already left. He spent the night in a hotel. Next day a local paper published a list of the passengers who had arrived by the *Empress of India*. The last name in the list read 'Mr S. Vivekananda'.

Arriving at Chicago Swamiji discovered that the last date for admission of delegates had expired. Further, he had no paper to show that he was being appointed to represent Hinduism. Last but not least, the hotel expenses were so exorbitant that the money that he had could not possibly last him for more than a few days. He seriously considered returning home and even asked his friends to send him some money for his return journey. This is hardly like a man who had felt he was on a divine mission.

As the cost of living in Chicago was high, he decided to move to a cheaper place. Perhaps he was not sure where he was going to go. As he was travelling on a train, a lady invited him to her place. This proved the turning-point. From here the drama moves fast. He soon returns to Chicago and speaks at the Parliament of Religions. At once the West recognizes here is a man with a message for it. The message builds, according to Tagore, a bridge between East and West, between ancient wisdom and the latest technology.

SPIRITUALITY

Once a Western critic said, 'It is easy to be spiritual in India: If you make a mess of your life, you are spiritual.'

This is not correct. It is easy to succeed in worldly matters, but it is extremely difficult to succeed in your search for spiritual illumination. A certain amount of intelligence and hard work may ensure success for a person to earn money and live a fairly comfortable life. You do not need to be a genius to be an important person in society; often a very mediocre person comes to the limelight without doing or being anything important. That is certainly not the purpose of life.

What is the purpose of life? The purpose of life is to be useful to society. Each individual in his own way should try to contribute to the welfare of others. You may help society materially, or by merely being an extraordinary person morally and spiritually. You may create a research laboratory, a big hospital, or a charity fund for the welfare of orphans. All this is wonderful work for which society will always remain grateful to you. You may also make a scientific discovery that will benefit humanity for all time to come or you may write a book that will be a source of inspiration for many centuries. All this is a way of promoting human welfare and it is work that makes life worthwhile.

But how about men like Buddha and Christ? They were poor, they were not learned; yet they were influential during their lifetime. Their influence has since increased. These humble men have influenced the world history. They have influenced man in all spheres of his life: art, literature, philosophy, his way of thinking. They are still influencing man. They influence not by what they do or say; they influence by what they are. They show the way for man to follow; they show the way to spiritual illumination, to blessedness.

There have been others like Buddha and Christ. Some of them are known to history, some of them are not known. They have come and gone, without attracting too much notice. They are like the dewdrops which nourish plants but are hardly noticed. They do not plan to do anything, but their presence is a blessing; it gives light, it sustains. A good man need not be a great man. A small man who is good and is willing to do others a good turn is better than an important man who lives for himself only. A society comprising small but good men and women is ideal.

To go back to the original question: How can a spiritual man be identified? What is spirituality? It is difficult to identify a spiritual man or define spirituality. Spirituality is what a spiritual man says or does. You may not be able to pinpoint the qualities of a spiritual man, but you know he is different from others. His likely qualities are: He is honest, he is also compassionate. He is a man above all barriers of race, religion, and language. He may not be rich, or politically important; yet he enjoys the love and respect of everybody. He does not claim that he has a following, but everybody tries to follow him. He gives much to society; of course he himself is the most precious gift. Any society will be proud to have a man like him. He is everybody's friend; everybody is his friend.

If such a person is not rich, or successful in the worldly sense, does it matter? Is society not the better for his failure in worldly matters? The world's assets are spiritual people, not those who are rich, learned, or politically powerful. Buddhas and Christs are few; the world needs more of them.

THE WAY OF THE GREAT SWAN

I t is said that if you give a mixture of milk and water to a swan, it will separate the two and drink only the milk. Impossible! you might say. The point is not if this is possible or not. Very likely, the swan does not possess any such capacity. The point is that this is a quality everyone should try to acquire. It is a quality of being able to discriminate, to separate the grain from the chaff, the good from the bad, the right from the wrong.

It may seem an easy thing to do, but it is most difficult, in practice. Ironically, to know what is right and to act according to that knowledge are two entirely different things. Few—indeed, very few—knowing what is right, are able to act in strict conformity with that knowledge. This gap between what we know and what we do is the source of all our troubles.

Wrongdoing is common at all levels of society. Not only the ignorant do things they should not do, the educated also do the same. When a man does something wrong, he does it from fear, in self-defence, or does it deliberately to gain some advantage, for instance. In either case, a wrong is a wrong. The circumstances do not justify the wrong, at best they may extenuate it. A truly conscientious man will never forgive himself for doing a wrong, though law or public opinion may take a lenient view of his act. Stealing is a crime, whether a poor man does it, or a rich man. But when a rich man does it, he does it not from necessity but from temptation. It is, therefore, all the more reprehensible.

The question is how a man can avoid doing wrong. The swan avoids the water and drinks only the milk. In the same way, why can he not avoid the wrong and do only what is right?

This is a question of practice. Every time we say or do something, we should ask ourselves if what we are going to say or do is right. If we think it is not right, we should avoid it, avoid it at all costs. It may be we have an opportunity to get what we have always wanted, yet we should reject it, reject it with contempt. Similarly, we may face loss of wealth or even life, yet we should not compromise, giving up the right for the wrong.

How can we have the strength to overcome temptation or fear? It is again a question of practice. To begin with, it seems impossible to resist even a small temptation. But if we are determined, we will succeed. Once we succeed, we gain self-confidence. The next time we face a similar temptation, we find it less difficult to overcome it. This is how we keep gaining our strength of mind and self-confidence. We have to be always alert so that we never give in to a temptation. We have to keep strict watch on ourselves. Somehow or other, we have to be our own master. We must not slip into a state of servitude to anything we hate. We need to make a habit of doing what is right. Buddha, in enunciating his eightfold path, keeps stressing righteousness: right thinking, right speech, right action, and so on.

Each of us has to behave the way a swan does, always discriminating, always making the right choice. Not only a swan, but a 'great' swan. Who is a 'great swan'? A man who is great in his effortless righteousness.

Happily there have been people who have shown the way how this can be achieved. Buddha was one such person, another was Christ. The fact that there has been one Buddha or one Christ is clear enough proof that the Great Swan is not a myth.

THE 1893 PARLIAMENT OF RELIGIONS

Columbus was looking for India, the El Dorado of every adventurous colonial power in those days, but hit America, instead. At first, he was disappointed, but soon his disappointment gave place to joy, for America was equally rich, perhaps richer. Soon Columbus' countrymen began to pour into the new land and settled wherever they found the soil rich and the climate mild. The British, the Germans, and other colonial powers followed suit. Sometimes, they fought each other and at one time, there was a civil war too, but finally they formed a federal government with a well-balanced distribution of powers between the Centre and the States. America is lucky in that it has had some remarkable men among its Presidents, who, with their vision and courage, have shaped the country into the richest and best governed one that America is today.

The people who had settled in the country had every reason to feel proud of their achievements. And it was natural that they wanted to show the world what they had achieved. They decided to have an exhibition where America's latest technologies would be on display. The exhibition was duly held. Never before had anything like this been seen. It was unique in terms of human ingenuity. It was called *The Columbian Exposition* in honour of the country's discoverer.

As an adjunct to this exhibition, a Parliament of Religions was also held. This too was unique, for it was the first time a meeting was held where representatives of different religions would meet and exchange views on religion. Some people say that the real purpose of the

Parliament was to demonstrate to the world that Christianity was the only true religion, or it was the best of all religions.

As the Parliament began, it looked like each delegate was eager to show how good his religion was. The only exception was the Hindu monk Swami Vivekananda, who said that each religion was equally good and capable of producing great men and women. He also said the attitude between one religion and another should be one of acceptance and not mere tolerance. Religions vary in details but they have a common goal and their essence is the same. They should, therefore, accept each other with love and respect.

The note Swami Vivekananda struck appealed to all and he became immensely popular. The American press paid him the highest tributes. It was struck by his wisdom, broad outlook, and oratory. Swami Vivekananda did not talk about any creed or dogma, he presented to his audience the rich tapestry of Indian culture. The West had so long believed that India was not only poor and backward, she was also uncivilized. The British were now trying to civilize the country. Ironically, Indians had the same idea about themselves. There were some among them who believed that the British rule was a blessing for the country. They thought everything British or Western was good and they blindly copied the West. Swami Vivekananda's success opened their eyes. They saw for the first time that there were areas in which India excelled the West. If they had to learn science and religion from the West, there were things like religion and philosophy which the West would do well to learn from India.

India's national resurgence may be traced to Swami Vivekananda's inspiration. He restored the country's sense of self-respect. But he was a citizen of the world. His concern was not for India alone but for the whole world.

THE RELIGION OF SWAMI VIVEKANANDA

Swami Vivekananda was certainly 'a Hindu monk of India' but he was a 'Hindu' in the broadest sense of the term. The word 'Hindu' was used by the Persians with reference to the people living across the river 'Sindhu'. Hinduism is the religion of these people. But the word 'Hindu' or 'Hinduism' occurs in no scriptures. The religion which now passes as Hinduism is derived from the Vedas. But it has undergone much change with the addition of many new beliefs and practices which it has assimilated over the centuries from many sources. The change has been so deep and extensive that it is no longer the same religion as the Vedas speak of. But this is not to say that the present Hinduism has completely deviated from the Vedas. The spirit remains the same but it expresses itself in different forms to suit different tastes. This flexibility has saved Hinduism even in its most difficult days. It has changed in details but its basic character has remained intact. The Vedas continue to inspire it, but it has drifted and is still drifting away from the mores characteristic of the past ages. It is ancient in its roots, but modern in its outlook.

Swami Vivekananda was not happy about the word 'Hinduism'. He would have preferred the word 'Vedic'. But by 'Vedic,' he meant the spiritual contents of the religion. The Vedas preach nothing but truth. Truth is one, but it can be variously explained. This brief statement sums up the infinite Vedas. The Vedas are no books, they are 'Knowledge', they are also known as 'truth'. The

Vedas are infinite because truth is infinite. Truth is everything. Truth is everything because it is impersonal. There is no way of describing truth. Truth is truth. Truth bridges the gulf between 'I' and 'you' or 'this' and 'that'. Truth is All. Truth is One. Truth is the Self of all, good or bad, big or small.

Swami Vivekananda preached no creed or dogma, he preached this truth. He called this truth the essence of the Vedas. It is in fact the essence of all religions. This truth is Hinduism to the Hindus, Islam to the Moslems, Christianity to the Christians. He called it Religion Eternal.

He described religion as a science. It is a science because it is based on truths which are verified and verifiable. If there has been one saint there can be many saints. Everybody can be a Buddha or a Christ. The goal of life is to be a Buddha or a Christ. Religion is the way to that goal. The path is not easy, but the goal is the highest that man can aspire to. No price is too high to reach that goal.

Swamiji preached only self-help. 'Try anything that works'—that was his advice. If a creed or dogma works, he would not mind it being tried. But he was against making a fetish of anything. He would not accept anything which was against reason. But he knew reason too was not infallible. Still, he would like a seeker of truth to use his own reason and blunder rather than be on the right path as a slave to somebody else.

According to Swami Vivekananda, the criterion of a religious man is his character. Is he honest? Does he feel for others? Does he treat everybody as his friend and relation? These are some of the things his character will reflect if a man is truly religious. Religion is the science which so transforms a man.

LIVING FOR A PURPOSE

Each individual has to decide what his priorities are and live accordingly. Food, clothing, accommodation, and a few other things constitute his essential necessities. He has to have them, but he also needs things not so much connected with the body. As the Bible says, 'Man cannot live by bread alone.' That is to say man's needs are not all physical but are also intellectual and spiritual. For instance, he needs music, art, literature, philosophy, and so on. He loves company. He loves nature. He loves to think and he tries to figure out how everything including himself came into being. Who created the world? Who rules it? A hundred and one such questions haunt him. Do those questions bother the animals? Do they have a mind? Probably not. If they have, it is a feeble mind. Man is supreme because of the power of his mind.

Even among men and women, there are some who possess superior mental faculties. They are more intelligent, have better memories, know a wide range of subjects, reason better, are more perceptive, and can express themselves better. Then, there are some who make new discoveries and invent things. They are in a class by themselves. So are also prodigies: musicians, painters, litterateurs, sportsmen, and so on. There are also original thinkers, people who give new twists to human thinking. They blaze a new trail, which other people follow.

This is how the human civilization has progressed. There have been people who have contributed to its growth at the material level, there have been others who have contributed to its growth at its moral level. Man was hardly better than an animal, to begin with. But once his mind took control of his behaviour, he began to grow by leaps and bounds. His growth has since then been ideological, rather than physiological. Not only his behaviour-pattern has changed and is changing, his concepts, attitudes, sense of right and wrong, values, everything concerning his mind is changing too. This process of change will continue. From gross to fine, that is how he is changing. His feelings and emotions, his imagination, his understanding of things—all these will grow finer and finer. There are already people who live more at the mental level than at the physical. Their identity is more in the mind than in the body. They withdraw themselves from the surrounding world and retire within themselves. They are alone with themselves. Are they happy? Judging from their behaviour, they are. If they are unhappy, it is not because of themselves, it is because of their fellow men. Such people, known as mystics, appear again and again.

The question is: Can man decide upon a goal and finally reach it? Or is his own effort no factor, but circumstances have jerked him into the position where we see him? Is genius nothing but a freak?

An intelligent man does not want to depend upon circumstances or destiny. He plans, makes efforts, and hopes to get what he wants. If he does not get what he wants, he does not blame anybody or anything, he blames himself. He resumes his efforts and tries with renewed vigour. He lives for a purpose and he does not want to waste time shedding tears over his failure.

'TRUTH MUST PREVAIL'

'Truth must prevail' is a declaration made by the Upanishads. But is it true? Does truth always prevail? It is, however, common experience that a dishonest man thrives whereas an honest man suffers in many ways. Few rich men are honest. The secret of their being rich is that they have no scruples about how they make their money. Other factors may help them, but what helps them most is the fact that their conscience is dead. Maybe their conscience pricked them when they first did something wrong. They might have felt uneasy that they had committed the wrong. They might have even felt nervous about being found out and punished. But, as it often happens, they got away with impunity. Next time they committed a similar wrong, they felt less uneasy. Their conscience did not trouble them much nor did the fear that they might be caught. Gradually they became more daring and began to commit one wrong after another without the least compunction. People might suspect them but these offenders soon learn how to keep a straight face and pretend that they are innocent. The public may come to know the truth but they dare not say a word against them, for these people are often well placed in society and are also influential. They can harm you if you dare go against them. The irony is that honest people are scarcely ever rich. Because they are not rich they have no influence over society. In modern society money and power go together. Those who are honest are often victims of injustice, but because they are poor they are helpless against the wiles of these unscrupulous and powerful people. Far from prevailing against the dishonest, they suffer at their hands.

Is the scripture then wrong when it says, 'Truth must prevail'? No. The scripture does not want you to follow truth for any gain. It wants you to follow truth for its own sake. You follow truth because there is no alternative to it, so far as you are concerned. Your commitment to truth should be total and unconditional. Whether you lose or gain, you are honest because you want to be honest. Honesty is both the means and the end for you.

The scripture does not want to tempt you when it says truth must prevail. It only makes a statement of fact. Truth surely prevails, but not in the way you expect. Truth prevails because truth is truth, because truth remains truth and falsehood remains falsehood, now and forever. Whether we recognize truth or not, it remains what it is. It is not the fault of truth that we do not recognize it, it is our fault. Someday or other, the truth may be known, but what if it is never known? It will remain what it is. Even if Galileo had not discovered the truth about the movement of the earth round the sun, the earth would have continued to move that way just as it had done in the past.

Truth will always prevail because it is not dependent on anything. It is not even limited by time and space. It is supreme. It is the principle round which everything else moves. Truth is universal and eternal; it is also impersonal. Everything else decays but not Truth. Truth is always the same, unchanging and unchangeable. It does not wait for anybody's recognition. Though the mills of God grind slowly, yet they grind exceeding small. Sooner or later, truth shall prevail. Truth is God and God is Truth.

THE GOOD AND THE PLEASANT

Things people run after in the world can be divided into two categories—the good and the pleasant. More people, however, incline towards the pleasant things because they can be attained more easily. Often you never get the good things though you try hard.

Take for instance, money. Money attracts everybody because it is the key to many pleasant things. If you have money you have almost everything you desire—food, clothing, comforts, power, honour, everything. No wonder, people want money most.

The things money can buy are easy to get, but it is difficult to acquire a moral virtue like honesty. There are plenty of rich people in the world but few people are truly honest. Not many people think it is important to be honest and only a few among them who so think succeed in being honest. The same is true of other moral virtues.

With a little intelligence and hard work it may be possible to acquire wealth. One in every hundred people is well-to-do, but not one in a million is honest. Many try, but they fail because the path is indeed very difficult. Trying to acquire a moral virtue is like climbing a hill. It is hard work. Those who are rich are rich because they are clever people—clever, hard-working, and practical. Why can't such people be also honest? What special effort has a man to make to be honest? And, above all, what is the hallmark of an honest man?

An honest man is one who never deviates from truth. 'He will sacrifice everything for truth but never sacrifice truth for anything.' Such people are pillars of society. No corporate life is possible where honesty is missing. If people cannot trust one another, a happy family or a society with abiding friendship among its members, is not possible. If the members of a family are each for himself, without any feeling for others, no one feels secure; each is afraid of the other. Can there be any civilization where there is no mutual trust?

For an individual what is good is his character. If he has a character morally rich, he commands respect from all. He may not own wealth or be a learned man, yet he will enjoy the love and respect of all. When he makes a comment people will attach importance to it. This is because what he says springs from the goodness of his heart.

What is pleasant is temporary, because it is not based on anything permanent. Flattery may be very pleasant but it comes from people who have a selfish motive. They flatter for some gain, but if they do not get what they want they may start finding fault with you. Similarly, health, beauty, power, and most other things in the world are pleasant but they are temporary. Sooner or later they decay. The good things are permanent. If you have a large heart it never shrinks. You feel for others though you may not be able to help them in the manner you would like. Love, friendship, and goodwill are hard to acquire but once you acquire them they are always yours.

If something is pleasant it is pleasant to you only and not to others. As a selfish person, you enjoy it and you are proud of it. A good thing is good, not for you alone but for all.

IN SEARCH OF GOD !
BETWEEN THE PEAKS AND THE PLAINS

He was 'Baba' to the orphans he looked after, 'Dandi Baba' to the neighbours. His brother disciples shortened his name Gangadhar to 'Ganga'. Swami Vivekananda, an expert in inventing nicknames, called him 'Ganges' or 'the Swami with a sword-shaped nose' in view of his pointed nose.

Ramakrishna's disciples were each in a class by himself, but Swami Akhandananda was special. He left home when he was barely eighteen. His father put him on board a train, saying 'I bless you that you may realize God.' Gangadhar's destination was the Himalayas. He had meanwhile met Ramakrishna, the God-intoxicated man, whose message to the world was to realize God somehow or other. This might have inspired Gangadhar to leave home in search of God. No authentic account of his travels in the Himalayas is known, but from his scraps of talks it appears that he not only traversed through the Himalayas but even went beyond into Tibet. His encounter with the lamas and his close brush with death at their hands on the suspicion that he was a British spy—he thrilled his audience when he narrated these incidents. For some years he had not been seen or heard of and many thought he was dead. One day, at Almora, Swami Shivananda discovered him in the company of Tibetan lamas and both began to weep when they recognized each other.

On his return from the West Swami Vivekananda preached what he called Practical Vedanta. The sum and substance of this philosophy is that everything is divine and we should therefore treat everything accordingly. While God is everywhere, it is in man that God is most manifest. We should, therefore, serve man as if we are serving God.

Once Swami Vivekananda had gone to Darjeeling to rest. While he was there, a plague epidemic broke out in Calcutta. People were in great distress and their condition was made worse by the repressive measures enforced by the alien Government. Swamiji rushed to Calcutta to try and see what relief he could arrange for the unfortunate people. When friends asked what he was going to do about funds he said he was prepared to sell the newly-founded Belurmath, if necessary. Sarada Devi intervened—and thank God he did not take that extreme step. Nivedita, Swami Akhandananda and Swami Sadananda started visiting the slums where the plague was raging. Nivedita issued appeals for volunteers. Scores of college students joined them in nursing the plague patients and cleaning the slums. The people of Calcutta saw for the first time Swami Vivekananda's Practical Vedanta in action.

When the plague relief ended Swami Akhandananda became restive to go back to the Himalayas. This time he decided to follow the course of the Ganges. As he approached Murshidabad he saw the ravages of a famine everywhere. Children surrounded him begging for food and he had literally to run away from them. But he had not gone far when he felt his body go numb and he had to stay. He took it as a signal that to see God he need not go to the Himalayas but that God was right before him in the poor and famished people around him. He started begging for the beggars and soon was able to feed people who would have otherwise gone without food. Many children had been rendered orphans by the famine and Swami Akhandananda became their 'Baba'.

THE TWO FRIENDS

They were close friends: Gadai and Chinoo. But never were two persons so unlike: Gadai, teen-aged, a brahmin, a school drop-out, carefree in his outlook on life; Chinoo, middle-aged, a shudra, owner of a grocery shop, very sedate, deeply religious. The story of Krishna and his many pranks absorbed him. No other religious character appealed to him so much.

Chinoo, alias Srinivas, lived in the same village as Gadai, but in a different neighbourhood. Gadai, that is, Gadadhar (later Ramakrishna) was also religious, but he loved not only Krishna, but every form of God. Whenever they met—they met often—they argued about religious matters. Chinoo had some fixed notions and tended to be dogmatic. Gadai loved to prove how hollow his notions were and made fun of his dogmatism. Chinoo, having read the *Bhagavata* well, knew the essence of the Hindu tradition. He rebutted Gadai's arguments with appropriate quotations from the *Bhagavata*, but Gadai always seemed to have an edge over him. Sometimes the argument continued for days together. Somehow or other Chinoo always found himself on the defensive, for Gadai, speaking from the common-sense point of view, made his stand look so vulnerable! Chinoo relied on his scholarship, but Gadai's weapon was his innate skill of argument, his sense of humour, and his quick repartees which often left Chinoo totally defenceless. He began to recognize the presence of some special power in Gadai which enabled him to separate the corn from the chaff. If ever Gadai found himself in a spot, he silenced Chinoo by climbing his shoulders. The argument stopped for the day, but only to be resumed at the earliest opportunity.

This continued for how long no one knows for certain. It must have continued a long time, judging from how Chinoo changed. Whenever they met, they argued as usual, but Chinoo began to feel he was losing ground to Gadai. Gadai spoke from wisdom the source of which Chinoo knew nothing about. The source was not books, it was something else. He spoke with authority which Chinoo could not deny. He might still argue but his argument had lost its force. He realized Gadai drew his inspiration from somewhere beyond his reach. He had previously felt unhappy if he could not cope with Gadai's arguments, now he felt elated. Whatever he said must be right. It was not an argument, it was a message.

At last, the final surrender came. Chinoo had become feeble and he knew his end was not far off. One day he invited Gadai to a thicket in the village. Few people even visited that place. He garlanded Gadai and then worshipped him in the formal way. Finally he dropped on his knees and with folded hands said, 'Lord, I know who you are. You are the saviour who comes again and again to show mankind the way. You are a boy, not many people know yet who you are and what you are in this world for. The time will come when people from all corners will rush to you for your blessings. I won't live to see that. But, Lord, please remember I was the first who recognized you. And please bless me.'

For once his friend did not contradict him. He also remembered him and often talked about him in later years.

THE ENCOUNTER

'Sir, have you seen God?' Naren, later Swami Vivekananda, put this question to Sri Ramakrishna on one of his early visits. He had seen Sri Ramakrishna in various moods; he had seen him also in ecstasies. He had heard him talk about God and as he did so he had the impression that God was right before him. But was He really? Had Sri Ramakrishna really seen God? Or was it his intense devotion which made him imagine that he had seen God? Naren was prepared to concede that Sri Ramakrishna was a very sincere man. But was he normal? Naren doubted it. Was he not suffering from some sort of mania so that he could not help talking of God all the time? Naren's argument was that if there was a God, then some people must have seen Him. So far he had not met a single person who could honestly say that he had seen God. Sri Ramakrishna, however, talked of God as if God was a reality; he had not only seen Him, he had also talked to Him. He addressed God as 'mother' and he behaved as if She was his real mother: He demanded constant attention from Her and if he did not get it, he was disconsolate.

Naren thought Sri Ramakrishna was the fittest person to answer his question. He put the question 'Sir, have you seen God?' as if he was challenging Sri Ramakrishna to prove his bona fides. Sri Ramakrishna's answer was prompt and clear : 'Yes, of course I have seen God. I have seen Him as clearly as I see you. And if you so wish, I can show Him to you too.' This was much more than Naren had expected. In saying, 'I can show God to you,' Sri

Ramakrishna had thrown down the gauntlet. Could he pick
it up? Naren must have felt that he had at last met his
match. A biographer has described him as a powerful bull
charging a frail man, Sri Ramakrishna. The latter held him
by the horns and made him fall at his feet 'in grateful
surrender'.

It is true that Naren finally surrendered, but the tussle
between the two lasted long. There was a time when Sri
Ramakrishna stopped talking to Naren, whom he loved so
much. Naren, however, kept visiting him as usual. Sri
Ramakrishna asked him why he came when he did not talk
to him. Naren's reply was characteristic : 'I come because
I love you, but please do not expect me to accept anything
and everything you say.' That was not Sri Ramakrishna's
wish either. He would not have anyone accept a statement
because it came from him. He liked Naren because he had
a questioning mind. Naren had surrendered to Sri
Ramakrishna but that did not deter him from challenging
Sri Ramakrishna's statements if he thought they were not
correct. The Master furnished appropriate proof and
silenced Naren.

When Sri Ramakrishna said to Naren, 'Yes, I have
seen God,' he was in fact addressing himself to a whole
generation of Indians, who, under the influence of
Western education, had begun to reject everything
Indian including the belief in God. In removing Naren's
doubts he was removing the doubts of the generation
that Naren represented. He stood between India and the
Western tide of agnosticism. He symbolized the best of
ancient India. Naren found nothing in Sri Ramakrishna
to which he could object. To his surprise Sri
Ramakrishna was like anybody else, but nobody was
like him.

FREEDOM IN BONDAGE

According to the Hindu scriptures, the ideal man is he who is in the world but not of it. That is to say, he is a person who does everything he is required to do, but he does not feel that he is doing anything.

Is such a thing possible? If a person is doing anything, how can he escape the feeling that he is doing something or other? It is ridiculous to suggest that he will not feel that he is doing anything. If he feels that way, he cannot be a normal person. Something must be wrong with him.

What is the idea the Hindu scriptures are trying to project? They are trying to say that you should have no wish of your own. If you do something, try to feel that God is the doer and not you. You are a mere tool at His hands; He is using you as He thinks best. You make a complete surrender to God and you are happy that He is making use of you.

This can happen only when you are totally selfless. That is to say, you are a person who lives for God, or if you prefer, for others. Because you are selfless, you have no wish of your own except to please God or do some good to others. You expect no reward, your only concern is to do your best. Having done that, you are happy.

The Hindu scriptures say that if you work with a selfish motive, there is no end to your worry. You start worrying right from the moment you begin your work;

you worry even if you are not doing anything. A selfish man is unhappy because he cannot bear to see the world not going the way he wants. He always has a feeling that he is surrounded by forces intent on hurting him. He is naturally unhappy.

Religion is nothing but selflessness. You are an ideal man if you live for others. When can you live for others? When you see God in others. In serving them you feel you are serving God. Unless you see God in others, you are not able to serve them selflessly.

Self-effacement is the *sine qua non* of religion. A truly religious man never thinks of himself, he thinks of others. He is happy if others are happy; if they are unhappy he is unhappy. Religion tells you to push aside your self and install in its place God. If you can do this, you are no longer responsible for what you do. If you do anything, you feel you are not doing it, the Lord is doing it through you.

Assuming it is possible for anybody to feel that way, how does it help him? The purpose of religion is said to be salvation. There is in all of us the feeling that we are not free and we struggle all our life to be free. Religion shows us the way to be free. The way is not to be attached to anything in the world. You are in the world but you are not of it. Since you are no part of it, the world cannot bind you, you are free. You may appear to be in bondage because you are in the world, but because you have no feeling of 'I' and 'mine', you are free. Freedom, which is the goal of life, is a matter of your feeling. If you feel you are free, you are free; if, on the other hand, you feel you are in bondage, you are in bondage.

MILES TO GO

'It is good to be born in a church, but it is bad to die there.' This is what Swami Vivekananda said to people who tend to get stuck at a certain point in the course of their search for God. They start with certain beliefs and they continue to stay with them to the end. This, according to Swami Vivekananda, was like a child beginning his education with a school primer and staying put there for the rest of his life. This surely is no sign of a keen and intelligent learner. This is a sign of someone who is intellectually and spiritually dying, if not dead already. A milder and less damaging interpretation, given by Aldous Huxley, is that it is as good as idolatry.

If you are an ardent seeker of God, you will certainly begin somewhere and with something to reach God, but you are not going to rest content if you find the methods you have adopted are not taking you forward as fast as you wanted. You will then start looking for other methods. You do not want to waste time. This does not mean that you are a restless person switching your methods every so often giving them no chance to prove their merits. This only means that you are in a hurry and you are a determined person who is not going to be satisfied with anything short of what he wants. This kind of impatience and this kind of insistence on having what he wants are conditions a seeker must fulfil in order to achieve the highest and best. If he cannot fulfil these conditions, he has to be content with less than what he wants. What he will get may even be less than what he deserves. There is no substitute for hard work. If you want to succeed, you have to pay its price in terms of hard work. Never did anyone succeed in a venture by a fluke only. You may have talents, but that will not assure success unless you work hard. You work hard not by fits and starts, but continuously, always, in the same manner, until success is fully in your grasp.

This you do not merely if you are a seeker of God, but in every venture, secular or spiritual. It may be easier for you to amass wealth, to be a first-rate musician, to write a great novel, to succeed in similar fields, given talent and hard work, but if you want to succeed in your search for God, you have to have not only talent and hard work, you have to have also the zeal that you are not going to stop till you reach the goal.

But what is that goal? Maybe it is not quite clear to you. Indeed, it can never be clear to you until you reach it. It is like climbing a mountain. You want to get on to the top of it, but you never know what the top is like until you get there. What do you do meanwhile? You keep climbing, climbing, and climbing. You may be tired; rest a little, but resume the climbing as soon as possible and continue till you are right on the top.

Life means struggle. Life means going forward. It means going on and on; you never stay stuck at one point. Be a river which is always on the move, always moving till it meets the sea. If the river stops moving it will stagnate and it will eventually die. Don't let that happen to you, you have miles to go. The goal? The goal is this going forward. It is an endless going and as you go you see new vistas of hills and valleys beckoning to you.

'LIFE IS BUT THOUGHT'*

In saying this Coleridge is echoing what Indian thinkers have always preached: 'You are what you think you are.' That is to say, your own estimate about yourself is largely an index of what you are now and what you want to be in the future. The present is always important because it is the foundation on which the future is built. The present may be clumsy and uncertain, but if you are clear in your mind about what you want to be in the future and if you organize yourself accordingly, there is no reason why you will not be what you want to be. Whatever may be your goal, you have to have the requisite will to achieve it and you have also to choose the right path. First ask yourself what you want and then start working to that end. There will be difficulties, but you brace yourself to face them squarely. Be sure you are never cowed by anything. If others have overcome such difficulties, you too can overcome them. If you have to form an estimate of yourself, you do not form it on the basis of what you are now and what you have so far achieved.

Look at persons of your calibre and study what they have achieved. It is by comparison that you learn what you are capable of. You discover to your surprise that most of those who have achieved great things in life are people of average merit and some—perhaps most—of them are markedly inferior to you. How is it that they have done so? By their will, by their own efforts. To begin with they never suspected what they were capable of, but as they

* S. T. Coleridge

started working hard, they slowly began to discover new sources of strength within themselves and their potential. Once they tasted success, they never looked back. They kept pushing forward from one success to another.

When you look at them and at their record of achievements, you feel tempted to follow in their steps. And if you are able to overcome your initial diffidence and make a start, you begin to feel that you too can succeed like others have done. The goal you have set yourself may be far away, but you never lose heart, never stop and never admit defeat. You keep trying, always, determined that you will not stop till you succeed.

But what is 'success'? It is difficult to give a definition to the word which will be acceptable to all. If your aim is not high and you achieve your aim, you think you have succeeded and you are pleased with yourself. To another person this is only the starting-point and he feels he has far to go. He in fact is never pleased with himself. He always wants to push forward and there is no point where he will stop and say, 'At last I have reached my goal.' If success means rest, there is no success for him.

Sri Ramakrishna would never like anybody to think he was good-for-nothing. He belonged to that school of Indian thought which says that there are infinite possibilities in man. The purpose of life is to fulfil these possibilities. He wanted everybody to believe that he could achieve what others have achieved. If anybody spoke of himself in condemnatory terms, he was most unhappy. Like most Indian thinkers, he was of the opinion that a man is what he thinks he is. It is his own thought which determines the course of his life and character. If you think you are going to be a saint, you commit yourself to that ideal and it becomes difficult for you to do anything by which you contradict yourself.

MOTHER AND SOME OF HER
FAVOURITE CHILDREN

Sarada Devi was 'Mother' to everybody in Calcutta, but in her own village, 'aunt' to most people. If anybody called her otherwise, there must have been a special reason for it.

According to records, those in her village who belonged to lower castes usually called her 'Mother'. It is difficult to explain why. Was it because they felt that way they could assert their claims on her more? Some of them surely felt she was their dearest and sincerest friend. Her caste, her age, her status—all these were no barriers : she was their Mother.

Take the case of Majhi Bou. An old Santhal woman, she often visited Mother and confided to her all her problems. It is not difficult to imagine what problems she talked about. Poverty, first and foremost. But there were other problems also. What passed between the two no one knows for certain, but as the interview drew to a close, Mother was seen handing her a few odd things—for instance, some food to eat on the spot, and some to carry home, a piece of cloth for her use and similar other things. To top Majhi Bou's troubles, she lost her only son, the stay of her life. She rushed to Mother to give the news. Mother completely broke down. She began to wail as if the bereavement was hers. Majhi Bou and Mother both started crying together. Mother had never been seen in such grief.

The story of Mother's weakness for the Moslem youth Amjad is well known. Amjad often landed in jail for committing thefts, yet he was always welcome to Mother. Once, after serving a term in jail, he came to see Mother, not in the least embarrassed about being in jail. Mother welcomed him and made anxious enquiries about his health. She invited him to stay for lunch and Amjad gladly agreed. Mother was ailing, so she asked one of her nieces to serve. Conscious of Amjad's character, the niece served food as if she were throwing it at him. Mother protested and, finally, herself began to serve. She knew that Amjad, her wayward son, needed care and affection more than anything else. As if to explain her conduct, she also added, 'Amjad is as much my son as Sarat (the highly respected disciple of Sri Ramakrishna) is.'

Once a young man of the lowest caste requested her to accept him as a disciple. Conscious of the caste tyranny prevalent in society. Mother put him off, making one excuse after another. She said things like 'I'll look after your spiritual progress. For this you don't need a mantra, all you need is to come here from time to time.' But the young man was adamant; and Mother would not also relent. Finally the young man came up with the question, 'How come you had no objection to being a daughter to a man of my caste in the past, but now you object to being my Mother?' The young man was grandson of the Bagdi couple Mother met long back on her way to Dakshineswar. They were robbers, but they were moved by Mother's manners. They became and remained Mother's parents ever since. The young man was obviously referring to that incident. This settled the issue and Mother accepted the young man as her disciple.

DIVINE DISCONTENT

In some circumstances it may be good to be content with what you have, but it is never good to be content with what you are. You may not have much money, a high social status, any political power, much learning, and so on. That is to say, you are a humble person with nothing by which you can draw public attention. People in the neighbourhood hardly know anything about you, or see any reason to want to know who you are, and what you do. In short, you are an insignificant person whose presence is not felt outside the limits of his family.

But are you unhappy about this anonymity of yours? Is this anonymity a thing of your choice, or a by-product of your circumstances? If your anonymity is self-imposed, people will raise their eyebrows and ask, 'Is the man normal?' If it is because of your circumstances, no one will make any comments. In a society where a man's worth is judged by money or such other criteria, no wonder you are a non-entity. And most people in the world are non-entities. But that is not to say they accept the situation without demur: They keep grumbling to the last day that society has not been fair to them. Their discontent is of a different kind: It flows from what they do not have.

But what about those who are anonymous by choice? Are they happy? No, they are also unhappy. They are unhappy because they are not what they want to be. But why do they prefer anonymity? They are like artists who feel they can use their talents best if they live away from crowds, away from the glare of name and fame. They want to spend most of their time in the pursuit of the art of their choice. Every minute is precious to them. They will be grateful to you if you leave them alone so that they can use their whole time for their art.

But what is *their* art? The art of 'being'. They are already good, but they want to be better, they want to be perfect. Money, power, beauty, name and fame—these are nothing to them. Their only concern is how to attain perfection.

Suppose you are a person trying to be perfect. What are the steps you take? First imagine yourself as a sculptor trying to produce a good Buddha. You begin with a chunk of stone and keep working on it with your chisel and hammer. You work day and night. Nothing is more important to you than this work. People may misunderstand you, even your close relations may think you crazy, but you do not care. The only thing that matters to you is the Buddha you are trying to produce. You want a perfect statue, as perfect as that holy man was, if not better.

You think you are the chunk of stone and you are working on it so that you may be as perfect as Buddha. Everything you do, mentally or physically, is directed to this end. You keep telling yourself that you are not going to be content with anything short of perfection. The whole world may say that you are already a Buddha, but you pay no heed to this praise. You never feel content with yourself. You have a discontent that keeps pushing you forward all the time.

This is what is called 'divine discontent'.

THE BRIDGE

Tagore said, Swami Vivekananda tried to build a bridge between the East and the West. What exactly did Swami Vivekananda do to justify this statement? Swami Vivekananda was a true citizen of the world. Being a non-dualist, he saw no difference between the East and the West; he saw the world as one. His home was everywhere, everybody was his brother or sister. He saw the same God everywhere, in everything, in every being. He believed in the oneness of things and this belief was the outcome of an experience every mystic aspires to but few, very few, indeed, attain. Swami Vivekananda had attained it and this is why he was able to see God in the wicked as much as in the holy.

To him man was an image of God. The best way to worship God was to worship Him in man. According to him, man was the 'living' God, the God who understands you and answers your questions. He is infinite, but for your sake has become finite, has assumed a form so that you may worship Him. Every form is His form, black or white, tall or short. He who is formless has assumed manifold forms so that you have no difficulty in recognizing Him and worshipping Him in the form you like best. In Him there are no relatives, there is only the Absolute.

'Having known this oneness do whatever you like,' said Sri Ramakrishna. What Sri Ramakrishna meant by this was that if you realized this oneness, you would see everyone as your own and every place as your home. This is why the East and the West were the same to Swami Vivekananda. He was as much a man of the West as of the East. Wherever he was he felt at home — as if he was among his own people. The people too felt he was one of their own and they treated him as such. His success as a religious teacher was largely due to this reciprocal love and trust.

Swami Vivekananda had great admiration for the West for its achievements in science and technology. His first acquaintance with Western technology was at the breath-taking Columbian Exposition. He visited the Exposition again and again, admiring everything he saw there. The Exposition confirmed his belief that man was only next to God.

His next surprise was the American heart. Miss Sanborn offered him, a chance acquaintance from the weird East, a home when he had none. She also made it possible for him to attend the Parliament of Religions. The next surprise was Mrs Hale who offered him not only a home but also motherly love. As in America, so also in England he had the same warm reception.

While Swami Vivekananda praised the West for many things, he was disappointed to find the people, by and large, indifferent to the higher values of life. He felt India could fill in this vacuum by sharing with them her spiritual experiences. Swamiji was for science and technology, but without religion the circle would not be complete. Physical well-being was certainly desirable, but more desirable was a morally and spiritually strong character. Swamiji wanted India to learn science and technology from the West and wanted the West, in return, to learn religion from India. In other words, he wanted to unite Indian religion with Western science and technology. No one advocated this unity more passionately than he. He truly stood as a bridge between the East and the West.

The *Katha Upanishad* talks of a '*setu*' (bridge) that spans the gulf between the secular and the spiritual. Swami Vivekananda was that '*setu*' for all.

HUMAN FACE DIVINE*

If you have good thoughts in your mind, your face will show it; if you have bad thoughts, that too the face will show. This is why the face is said to be the mirror of a man's heart.

But is this always true? What if a man tries to hide his feelings? He may smile but inwardly he may have anger and hatred. He smiles only to deceive you so that you may not suspect his evil designs. To a shrewd observer the smile will look like a grimace, but an innocent person will be taken in by it. The face of a person often determines your future relations with him. 'Love at first sight' is not an exaggeration. You meet a person and at once you begin to like him. His face tells you he is a good man and you think what his face tells you is right. Your first impression may not be correct, still you go by the first impression until something happens that forces you to change your opinion.

But a man is not always the same. He may change and with that his face also may change. Let us say your first impression of him was bad because his face told you so. But he may have started changing since you first saw him and the change may have been much more enormous than you thought possible. He looked savage but now he is quite human. You see the change in his face. His face is changing, changing from savage to

---

* *Paradise Lost*, III. 40.

human, from human to divine. Hindu yogis seek unity with God and they attain it. When they attain that unity, they are no longer human, they are divine.

They are divine not only in character but also in physiognomy, in the face most of all. Looking at a true yogi, people will stop and ask themselves : 'Who is he, a man or God?' His face will glow with the beauty of the spirit. If they have any evil intent, a glance at his face will remove it from their mind. It will also give them comfort if they are in pain, courage if they are gripped with fear. The yogi need not say anything, his mere presence will inspire the best thoughts in others.

The most expressive part of the human body is the face. It is a vivid record of a man's life and character. Behind every line, every crease in the face is the story of his hard struggle, sometimes marked by success, sometimes by failure. If a man has a divine face, it must be that he worked hard over the years and succeeded in overcoming all that was ugly and base in him.

Buddha's face is a testimony to his nirvana. It shows the tranquillity that follows a storm. Buddha overcame the storm within and finally attained the peace 'which passeth all understanding'.[1] He conquered himself first and then conquered the world. The world needs men and women trying to conquer themselves.

The human face has to change into the divine face. That is the message of history, also of the men and women who create history.

---

1 Phil. 4 : 7.

'WHOSOEVER WOULD BE GREAT,
LET HIM BE SERVANT OF ALL'

Everyone wishes to be a leader, forgetting that to be a leader he has to be the humblest in the group to which he belongs. It is wrong to think that a leader is born; he is a person who works hard and climbs one rung after another till he reaches the top of the ladder. He may have been born with some special qualities which marked him out for leadership, but the most important among these qualities must have been his readiness to sacrifice his own interests for the sake of others. He surely had some good qualities so that in group activities his choice as leader was automatic and unanimous. But if he is a selfish man he is not likely to retain his position for long, he will be thrown out sooner or later.

There is an interesting story about Lenin: Soon after the Soviets captured power in Russia, the food situation, which had been bad earlier, became worse. People had nothing to eat except potatoes. Naturally there was much discontent throughout the country. This discontent was fuelled further by the rumour that though there was hardship for everybody, the leaders lived a comfortable life. They had everything they wanted. A group of people decided to pay a surprise visit to Lenin when he was having his lunch. They were taken aback when they discovered Lenin's only food was potatoes! Lenin asked them what they wanted. They said, 'We wanted to ask you a question. We have, however, found the answer to the question and we don't now need to put it to you.' Abashed, they left the place. No wonder the Soviet people still love and admire Lenin though they are disillusioned about Stalin, disillusioned even about Communism which Lenin had introduced.

The leader must be an example of what he preaches. People will love and respect him when they see he is an honest man true to what he stands for. If he betrays his professed ideals, people will hate him. Very soon, people will remove him from his position.

A true leader does not seek power, but power comes to him all the same. People love and respect him because of his character—and they follow in his footsteps willingly, gladly. Gandhiji never claimed that he was a leader. He never wanted people to follow him blindly, unthinkingly. He asked them to follow others if they thought they showed a better path. He also said he himself would follow that path if anybody could convince him that that path was truly a better path. His humility, his frankness—and, above everything else, his sacrifice endeared him to everybody. Even people who did not see eye to eye with him on many issues would gladly concede that he was indeed a great man.

A true leader does not place himself before others, he places others before himself. He does not want power and position, he only wants an opportunity to serve others. If he has power and position, he uses them only to serve others in a bigger and better way. He does not think he is the master, he thinks he is the servant of all. He does not claim any privilege, he only begs that he may be allowed to serve. He does not want adoration, he wants criticism so that he can avoid errors. If he commits an error for which people suffer, he repents. Gandhiji went on a fast if he erred. This sometimes led him to the brink of death. But this was his way of practising penance.

'NO ONE CAN BE PERFECTLY FREE
TILL ALL ARE FREE'*

It is difficult to conceive a world where all are equal, yet equality has been man's dream from the beginning of history. But what is equality? Does it mean sameness? Does it mean that we all will look and be the same? Is that possible, or desirable? If we are machine-made, we may be alike, but we are not machine-made. In fact, no two humans are alike, physically or otherwise. Each individual is unique. The question of equality between one individual and another does not arise.

What is meant by equality, then? Obviously equality means equality in terms of rights and privileges. All individuals and all nations should be treated alike. There should be no discrimination on grounds of religion, race, or colour. But some nations have also suffered and are still suffering because they are weak. The stronger nations exploit them but they get away with it just because there is no one to check them. Ultimately, the saying 'Might is right' prevails. The kind of equality which we foresee is still a far cry.

But there can be no real peace in the world unless there is equality. The weak are still afraid of the strong. They are not free, they are mere pawns in the hands of the strong. Everywhere, in every society, the minorities feel insecure. They are deprived but they are not always

* Herbert Spencer

able to voice their grievances. They suffer silently. There are international forums supposed to serve as guardians of peace. But do or can they maintain peace with justice? Doubtful. How impartial they are is questionable. The forums are useless if they do not function as the conscience of the entire human race.

Equality as a principle is universally accepted. What is needed is its enforcement. Everywhere the weak are neglected today. Even within the family the strong rule over the weak. Physical strength or money-power gets the upper hand everywhere. What is the way out? How can at least a semblance of equality be enforced? Those who are strong must recognize that it is in their interests to welcome equality. They have to take the initiative to see that the weak and strong all enjoy equal rights and privileges. They must understand they can never enjoy anything unless others are also enjoying it. They love freedom, but they cannot enjoy it for long if others are not enjoying it too. It is no freedom if it is freedom for a few only. Freedom must be for all. The days are gone when one race ruled over another, or one country ruled over another. In principle, all are free today, but in practice some are more free than others. Real freedom rests with the strong. But they can never be comfortable if others enjoy only limited freedom or none at all. The world is one and mankind is also one. There can be no peace unless there is freedom for all. A single individual in bondage is a threat to the freedom of all. Either all are free or none at all. Equality cannot be divided, it has to be one single whole; it has to be for all.

RELIGION AND PHILOSOPHY

Scholars sometimes raise the question : 'Which is more important, Religion or Philosophy?' Most of them think philosophy is more important, for it is based on experience. You observe facts, then you begin to ask yourself why those facts happened, why they happened the way they did and what they signify. After weighing everything you reach certain conclusions and it is these conclusions which constitute what is called philosophy. Philosophy is, therefore, objective and logical.

Philosophy is a system of rules and principles which try to explain the facts we observe. These rules and principles are all products of our own intellect, unless we recognize that there is such a thing as divine agency which is supreme. It is on this issue of divine agency that philosophers divide into two groups, one group believing that there is a divine agency and this divine agency determines everything, and another group believing that the so-called divine agency is non-existent or if it exists at all, it is indifferent to what happens in the world. Scholars argue that the first group cannot be taken seriously, for whenever they are in difficulty, they take refuge in an unknown power called God. But the position of the second group is still more vulnerable, for their observation and reasoning, the bases of their stand, vary from person to person.

Scholars are, however, suspicious of the bona fides of religion, because they think that religion is belief. It cannot be taken seriously, for it does not explain, it only wants you to take things for granted. How can you trust such a thing?

But religious people claim that religion is also a science. It is not a belief, it is an experience open to all. Just as in the case of physical science, you have to fulfil certain conditions to arrive at a given result, similarly in the case of religion you have to fulfil certain conditions in order that you can attain the desired experiences. You have to have deep concentration of the mind, work hard, and so on. More important, you have to have moral qualities like honesty, good will and love for all, self-restraint, and so on. You choose some great soul, say Buddha or Christ, as your ideal, and you try your best to be like him. It is not easy, but you keep trying and you never stop till you succeed. You are like one of those mountaineers who is determined to conquer the highest peak of the Himalayas. You stumble again and again, you get bruised all over, yet you are still determined to push on.

A religious man is not trying to attain anything outside: gold, power, or position. He is only trying to *be* like the man he has chosen as his ideal. He knows it is not easy, but he finds joy in trying and he keeps trying. If religion includes belief, it is the belief that such a goal is worth trying to achieve. He may never be another Buddha or Christ, but the fact that he is trying to be like them is a reward in itself. There is no miracle in religion; there is instead hard work, determination, and single-minded zeal. The goal of religion is perfection.

The difference between religion and philosophy is that while religion achieves, philosophy explains.

THE COBRA BITE

The Cobra, said to be the deadliest of all poisonous reptiles, catches a frog and kills it almost instantaneously. The frog may faintly protest a few times but within minutes it is silent because it is dead. The same frog, if caught by a rat snake, goes on protesting, loudly and a long time, before death comes and it is silent.

Narrating this, Sri Ramakrishna compares a good spiritual teacher to a cobra and a bad spiritual teacher to a rat snake. A good spiritual teacher has no difficulty leading his disciple to God; the disciple too has no difficulty following his teacher. Both play their respective roles with exquisite skill and beauty. The bad spiritual teacher, on the other hand, is slow and inefficient. He has taken on himself a task for which he is least fitted. As a result, he and his disciple both are in trouble, the teacher leading his disciple and the disciple following his teacher. It is like a blind man leading another blind man. They end up getting nowhere.

A spiritual teacher is a perfect man. He teaches by his example, by what he is. He is like a lamp that gives light to all including itself. He himself may be silent, but his life and character speak for him. He himself is shy, withdrawn, and not in the least keen about teaching others. He may even resent being addressed as 'teacher'. He would much rather be treated as a 'student' than as a 'teacher', and if there is anything to learn from anybody or anywhere, he will gladly learn it. If people still flock to him, it is because they are fascinated by his qualities. They think those qualities are extraordinary.

But what sort of qualities are they? The quality that distinguishes him most is honesty. He is honest because he is honest, not because of any hope of reward, or fear of punishment. He is honest because he cannot help being honest. If you want to know what honesty means and you want to be honest yourself, you make him your ideal and follow him in every respect. He becomes your teacher, so far as honesty is concerned, whether he admits it or not.

Next to honesty is the quality of love for all which distinguishes a spiritual teacher. He loves all irrespective of everything. He may love even his enemy; in fact, he recognizes nobody as his enemy, everybody is his friend and he is concerned for everybody. This is his nature, whether you like it or not. He is one of those impractical (according to us) persons who if hit on one cheek would turn the other.

But if he is such a simple and innocent person, how can he be compared to a cobra? How can his teachings be as effective as the bite of the cobra? The comparison is justified in the sense that he inspires people by his character and not by his words. He so inspires others that those who come in contact with him begin to change, eventually becoming exactly as he himself is. The change takes place in spite of themselves. The change is deep, permanent, and inevitable. It is like a lamp lighting another lamp. It is like pouring oil from one pot to another.

Such a teacher stands out like a big banyan tree in the midst of small trees. His strength is in what he is and how he influences others. He changes not only some individuals, he changes generations of people. The cobra is a small creature, but its power is immense. Similarly, the ideal spiritual teacher may be a humble person, but his benign power spreads far and wide, changing vast masses of people effortlessly.

CULTURE

It is difficult to define culture, for it is not an object, but a quality or a number of qualities. These together lend an individual or a society a distinctive character. It is this 'character' which is the culture of that individual or society.

What are the qualities that make up this character? There may be a difference of opinion about this, but undoubtedly, honesty is the first and foremost quality you would expect in a cultured man. It is difficult to imagine a cultured man who is not honest. It is said that 'a man of culture is rare'. A man of culture is rare because a truly honest man is also rare. Next to honesty is compassion which a man of culture is expected to have for everybody. His compassion cuts across all barriers of country or religion. He may even be sympathetic to a person branded by everybody as wicked, or even to someone inimical to him personally. The cultured man is kind because it is his nature to be kind. He loves everybody irrespective of whether the man he loves is good or bad, friendly or unfriendly to him, known or unknown to him.

Modesty is another quality that distinguishes a cultured man. He is polite to everybody, young or old, rich or poor. You may hurt him by your behaviour, but he will not retaliate. He will try to understand what he has done that you thought it fit to hurt him the way you did. He will blame himself rather than blame you. Similarly, suppose you ask him to do you a favour, but he is not in a position to do you that favour. Either it is not within his power, or it is not moral. He is forced to say 'No' to you and he does say it, but he says it in such a way that it would seem that he is more disappointed than you are that he is not able to help you in your difficulty.

Culture is not in your looks or clothes, in your wealth or scholarship, in your heredity or political standing. Culture is in what you are. It is the radiance emanating from within yourself. It is the natural and spontaneous beauty of your life and character. It is the expression of what you have accumulated within yourself through years of struggle to attain the best, the highest, the most beautiful. You are like a flower plant drawing the best in itself and in the environment around it and transforming them together into the beauty and the fragrance of its flowers. Culture is yourself at your best. You may have flaws, but they only heighten your merits.

A country's culture is the culture of its people. In India, culture means right thinking, right speech, and right action. Love, goodwill for all, humility, charity, treating all alike, service, and selflessness—these are the basic qualities you would expect in a cultured man. Nothing is secular in India, everything is spiritual, whatever you do is an offering to God. It is true in the case of an individual and it is true also in the case of the nation as a whole. India's art, architecture, music, literature—everything representing the collective effort of the nation—is dedicated to God, that is, to the sum total of all men and women. A huge building but ugly, a big, powerful country but without scruples and always using its power to exploit others, are both in the same category. The stale word goodness is what is needed. Goodness has to be seen, it has also to be effective; goodness for its own sake, totally unconditional.

Culture is being good, doing good, irrespective of everything.

EDUCATION : HOW AND WHERE IT FAILS

Education is not book-learning; it is a way to perfection. You may have read much, but what sort of person you turn out to be from this reading is the question. If you are a better person in the sense that you use your education not only for yourself but also for the good of others, that is true education. But what if you use your knowledge for yourself only, and that, too, not in a very fair way? People will fear you but never trust you. They will begin to say that you are selfish and dishonest. What good has your education done for you, then ? You are no better than those who have never been to any school. You are even worse than they are.

True knowledge is like fire which consumes all impurities in the mind. First and foremost, it makes you honest and loving. The purpose of education is to help you acquire true knowledge, that knowledge which gives you a sound moral character. What you learn from books, teachers, or from other sources is important to the extent that it helps you to improve yourself. You may be poor, you may not be a great scholar, you may not be a child of a reputed family, yet you are happy with what you are and what you have. People around you may have amassed wealth by unfair means, but you are never tempted to do the same. You do not envy them, nor do you speak ill of them. You love and respect everybody, even such people. High or low, rich or poor, everybody is your friend. To you, truth is above everything else. No fear, no temptation, can make you deviate from truth. Similarly, you will never hurt others. Others may hurt you, but you will not retaliate.

An educated man is modest. He never boasts, never lets others know of his education, his character, his status in society, or his personal achievements in various fields. He is perfectly at home in whatever company he may be. If he is in the midst of village rustics, he will behave as if he himself is a village rustic. If they are talking about things they do not know much about and they are again and again making mistakes, a truly educated man is in no hurry to correct them. Even if they ask his opinion, he will, with great modesty and with as few words as possible, tell them what he knows. In doing this, he will give the impression that he is just like one of them and if he knows anything more than what they know, it is as if by some accident that he knows it.

Such a person is equally at ease in the midst of children. He has their simplicity and innocence. Children freely ask him questions and he also freely asks them questions, as if both are trying to learn from each other.

Today we sometimes meet so-called educated people who are vain, selfish, and dishonest. Education has been self-defeating in their case. They have degrees, but no character, which is the essence of education. But what is character? Character is honesty and goodness. If a man has never been to school and yet has these qualities, he is an educated person.

True education produces that kind of knowledge which makes you a better individual, better in every respect, specially morally. The first requisite for a better world is better men and women. Material prosperity is necessary, but more necessary are morally strong men and women. 'Education for all' is a good slogan, but what kind of education? It must be education that turns out intelligent and hardworking men and women who feel for others and who place others before themselves.

BUDDHA

Buddha was born Prince Gautama of the Shakya clan on the border between Nepal and India in the 6th century B.C. It was a time when in India religion had degenerated into mere ceremonialism or hot disputations about metaphysical issues. No one seemed to know what religion was about. Disgusted, Gautama left home in search of true religion. He met many teachers, but no one impressed him as a true holy man. He arrived at Gaya and chose a quiet spot under a banyan tree, where he sat to meditate. He resolved to perish there if he could not realize what he was seeking, the truth behind religion.

It took him some time, but he did at last realize the truth he was seeking. He became 'Buddha', the Enlightened. And, out of his infinite grace, he decided to teach people in the simplest possible language the truth that he had discovered. Going over to Sarnath near Benaras he 'set in motion the wheel of his dhamma.' As he walked through villages and towns preaching, people of all classes followed him.

What did he teach? First, he taught the four truths with which all of us are familiar: *dukha* (suffering), *dukha-samudaya* (there is a cause of suffering), *dukha-nirodha* (suffering can be prevented), and *dukha-nirodhini-pratipat* (the way to prevent suffering).

Buddha attached great importance to *Dukha Samudaya.* It is a truism, for it says there must be a cause behind an effect. If you want to remove the effect, you have to remove the cause. Why do you suffer? You suffer because of your improper and immoderate desires. Control your desires and your suffering will go. Self-control is in fact the foundation of true religion. *Dukha Samudaya,* known as the Law of

Dependent Origination in the scholastic world, occupies the key place in the message of Buddha.

Buddhism places on you the onus of determining your fate. You are responsible for what you are, or what you are going to be. There is no God in the Buddhist scheme of things; it only concerns itself with *you,* what you are and what you do. Be right and do what is right—that is the essence of Buddhism. This, presented in more detail, is what is known as the eightfold path.

Buddha was averse to philosophical discussion. If anybody raised a philosophical issue, he would refuse to give an answer. He would ask the questioner, 'What is important to you when you are shot with an arrow? Do you want the arrow removed and some medication for your wound, or do you want to know first the caste of the man who shot the arrow?' His approach to religion was entirely pragmatic. Religion is to give you relief from your suffering and not to lead you into a labyrinth of high philosophical argumentation.

Buddha's teaching was primarily for the ordinary man. He avoided scriptural jargon and taught in the language of the people. But he attracted scholars as much as he attracted the illiterate. His religion was for all, brahmin or non-brahmin. It was for all people of all time.

Buddha avoided philosophy, but the consequence of this has been that many schools of philosophy have now sprung up around him. It is still being debated whether Buddha taught a new religion altogether, or a revised version of Hinduism. The consensus is that he taught Hinduism, but Hinduism without the accretions that had then accumulated on it. What he preached was Vedanta, though he never used the term. Buddha 'was born a Hindu, lived a Hindu, and died a Hindu,' according to a well-known scholar.

Buddha may be best judged by his last message: 'Be thou a lamp unto thyself.'

SELFLESS SERVICE

According to Vedanta, Self-knowledge is the highest goal of life. You may know all about the world, but if you do not know who you are, then that knowledge is useless; even your life is useless.

But where is the self? How do I know it? Vedanta says the self is within you, hidden inside your heart. It reveals itself to you when you have a pure mind. But what is meant by a pure mind? A pure mind is a mind which is free from the sense of ego. If you feel you are separate from others, with a distinct name and form, that means you are conscious of your ego. When you have this consciousness, you have an unclear mind and you are not able to see your self. The self will reveal itself to you when you are able to remove your ego altogether. The ego is like a layer of dirt on a mirror; remove the dirt and you will be able to see your self clearly.

But how do we remove the dirt, that is, the ego? The *Gita* says that the best way is to install God where your own ego has reigned. Whatever you did you did for yourself. But now you do it for God alone. When you work for God, it is not work in the sense we understand the word: It is worship, for here you want no return for yourself. You not only work for God, you also offer the work's results to God. This is a kind of *yoga* and the *Gita* recommends it highly for everybody, as it is the best way to kill the ego and be in constant communion with God. This is the way to make your mind pure—to be always in a state of God-awareness. The *Gita* reminds us that work does not mean only physical work but it also includes thought and speech. When it asks you to work for God, it means that you will always think of God, talk of God, and also do whatever you can physically to please God.

People work because they have desires, and they want those desires fulfilled by hook or by crook. The irony is that as soon as one desire is satisfied, another takes its place immediately. It is an endless process. It is like trying to extinguish fire with oil. The oil does not extinguish the fire, it only increases it. This is why Sri Ramakrishna used to say, 'Change the direction of your mind.' If your mind is now directed to sense-pleasure, force it towards God; do it in such a way that nothing else can come between you and God.

God should be your first and last concern; nothing else matters to you. It is for God alone that you think, speak, and act. If that is the way you live, then, nothing you do can be a bondage to you. Ordinarily work produces results, and the results constitute bondage. This is the normal law of work. But this law will not apply in your case because you are not working for yourself. Whenever you did anything for yourself, good or bad, you invited trouble. You got some results but those results limited your freedom, one way or another. But now that you work only for God or for others, you have a pure mind and you know your self. You know that you are pure Consciousness, and not the body, not the mind, not any other adjunct by which you used to identify yourself. The gap between you and God no longer exists; you are in God, with God and of God; you are God Himself. Yet you are always active doing good to others. You are the most selfless being because you have no self of your own; your self is the Self of all.

The service you render in this state is truly selfless service.

MOTHER INDIA

An American couple were on their first visit to Calcutta. They had heard and read much about India, but they had heard more about Calcutta. They had heard about its filth, beggars, and its people, the Bengalis, who claim they have a flair for art, literature, and Marxist politics. But they had also heard of Ramakrishna. India, specially Bengal, was holy to them because of its association with Ramakrishna. Of all places in India, Calcutta attracted them most because it was the scene of Ramakrishna's activities in the period when his spiritual powers were at their peak. It was here that he discovered the future Vivekananda and trained him for the role he played in later years as his successor. In a way, Ramakrishna and Vivekananda between themselves created a new India. They taught that man was next to God and that to serve man was to serve God Himself. They were pioneers in propagating religious harmony, the unity of mankind, and the necessity of diversity. The couple were fascinated by these two idealists. They came to India to see for themselves how far the message of these two persons had influenced the common people of India.

They had already been in many parts of India and they were then on the last lap of their tour. They were struck by the diversity of the people's languages, religious beliefs, physical features, their food habits, the way they dressed, and so on. Each state was like a country. Yet the states were together and they seemed to get on very well in spite of their differences. If there was a unity, it was something genuine and deep-rooted. It was not make-believe, or something superimposed. The visiting couple were impressed by what they heard and saw as they travelled through the country. They met people of all ages and all communities and were struck by the richness of their human qualities. They did notice their shortcomings, but they thought that with a little economic uplift the people would be able to overcome them. This was confirmed by an experience they had one day when they were out on a stroll. They noticed an old woman on the pavement, begging. She was blind and doubled up with age and poverty. With their broken Hindi they started a conversation with her. They first asked if she had anyone to look after her. She said, 'Yes, God.' The couple fell at her feet and said, 'You are Mother India.'

They are right, for India's spiritual outlook has remained the same despite all the ups and downs she has gone through over the centuries. To her, the ideal man is the man of God. You may not be rich, or a scholar, or a politically important person, yet you will be held in high esteem if you are truly religious. In ancient India, a sage was more influential than a prince. The prince ruled, but only as the sage dictated. Individually or collectively, people strictly followed what the holy man told them to do. 'Truth is above everything else'—that is what India has always believed. As a modern sage taught, 'You can give up everything for Truth, but you cannot give up Truth for anything.' Religion has been, and will always be, her backbone. Any attempt to replace religion will be suicidal. But what is religion? Religion is Truth and Love. There is no God where Truth is denied and Love is absent.

Let Mother India be poor, but let her love God and love His best creation—man.

MIND

What is the mind? It is difficult to define it. According to Hindu philosophy the mind is an organ which controls all other organs, the organs of action and perception. It is called the principal organ although it is invisible. It can be known only by its functions. It is inside the body but where it is located is controversial. The mind is, however, matter, according to Hindu philosophy.

The mind is so powerful that it is often considered the real identity of man. The mind is variously called: 'mind', 'intellect', 'heart', and 'I-ness' The designations are based on their different functions. 'Mind' is that state in which you cannot decide one way or another. That is, at one point you say you will do something; at another, you say you will not do it. You don't understand your mind; it is always wavering. But the mind can also be determinative. It examines the pros and cons and then comes to a decision. When the mind so works, it is called the 'intellect'. Another function of the mind is to feel. It feels pleasure and pain, joy and sorrow. It is also the seat of all emotions and the repository of all memories. When the mind works this way, it is called the 'heart'. There is yet another function of the mind, 'I-ness'. This I-ness characterizes everything the mind does. The mind says, 'I am the doer, I am the enjoyer, and so on.' This I-ness is individualism asserting itself.

According to Vedanta, the Self is supreme. It is everywhere and in everything. It is Pure Consciousness and it is this Consciousness which manifests itself in whatever the mind does. The mind acts through the organs, but it is

Consciousness which enables the mind to do whatever it does. Without this Self, without this Consciousness, the mind is dead and the body also is dead. When a person dies, all his organs may be intact, yet they do not work. This is because the Self, that is, Consciousness is gone. A jar has space in it just as there is space outside. But if the jar breaks, the space inside the jar merges with the space outside. There is then one space; there is no separate space any longer. Similarly, when a person dies, the Consciousness within the person leaves the body and merges with the Consciousness outside. Consciousness is always one and the same. The division inside and outside the body is artificial and false. Consciousness is the only reality; it is all-pervasive. The difference between one object and another is in the degree of its manifestation of Consciousness. An object is called inert if Consciousness is not manifest in it.

Where is Consciousness located in the body? Is it in the brain? Consciousness is everywhere in the body. It is, however, possible that it is more manifest in some parts of the body than in others. If the brain is damaged, there may be no manifestation of Consciousness. An individual with a damaged brain or a brain under-developed, is an idiot, a mindless person. Animals have brains, but their brains are immature and weak. They cannot think, discriminate, or argue; they also cannot imagine. They go by habit or instinct. The human brain is the highest. Science, philosophy, literature, and art are examples of what the human mind can create. The present civilization is proof of its capability.

But more significant is what the human species can achieve in terms of moral and spiritual qualities. Human beings can become Christs and Buddhas. All they have to do is to control the mind. When they do so, the perfection already in them manifests itself. This perfection, also called Pure Consciousness, works through the mind.

GOD AS MOTHER

God is beyond thought and speech, yet we wish to see Him, talk to Him, and seek His favours. But does He exist? We are not even sure of that, but we love to think that He does. Where? We do not know but we are told that He lives in Heaven. No one knows where Heaven is, but whenever people pray, they look upward as if Heaven is somewhere in the sky. God is in Heaven, but He keeps watch over everything going on down below on earth. He keeps track of what people do and He rewards or punishes them, depending upon whether what they do is good or bad. In brief, for most people God is a terror. He is a despot and He does whatever He likes.

Yet there are people who love Him. You may say this is no real love, for there can be no real love born of fear. It will be more correct to call it flattery. When you pray, you attribute many absurd qualities to God. That is nothing but flattery. You are fawning on Him in order that you may get His favours.

But is there no genuine love? Is love always selfish? No. There are plenty of people who love God without asking for anything in return. In all religious traditions you have mystics who love God more than they love themselves. They leave home, retire into the forests and suffer privations, only because they want to concentrate their mind on God. They do not want any worldly object from Him. If they want anything at all, they want only to love God. They beg that they may not succumb to any kind of temptation; all they want is that they may have pure love for God.

They are not afraid of God. If they have a misfortune, they will not say that they have offended God and He is, therefore, punishing them. Instead, they will say it is a blessing from God and they will thank Him for it. They believe whatever happens to them is ordained by God and it is good for them. At the most, they may pray that God will give them strength to bear their troubles.

Hindu mystics love to imagine that God is their dearest and nearest: He is their father, mother, or master. Of course the sweetest of all relationships for a mystic is that of mother and child. Such a mystic believes that God is his mother and he is her son. He is not afraid of his mother. Even if he commits a mistake, he will blame God for his mistake. He will say, 'Mother, you know I am foolish and ignorant. Why don't you take better care of me? Why do you let me do things I should not do?'

A typical example of this was Ramprasad, a mystic, who looked upon God as his mother. In one of his songs he threatens God because He is neglecting His duties as mother. He says he will sue Him for this. He will not agree to any compromise unless God takes him up in His arms.

In recent times Ramakrishna was another mystic who worshipped God as mother. In the course of his worship of Mother Kali, he began to wonder if Mother accepted his worship. He remembered how mystics in the past behaved : They ceaselessly cried for the vision of God. Ramakrishna started doing the same. He even tried to commit suicide. Finally God was pleased to grant him His vision. God not only became his mother, He also became his friend, playmate and constant companion. He and Mother Kali were always together, like a child and his mother.

Ramakrishna stands out as the best example of how you worship God as Mother, and how this transforms you.

WISDOM

The word *wisdom* implies something more than *knowledge*. We may have knowledge of something, but if we do not know how, where, and when to use it, that means we lack wisdom. Sri Ramakrishna used to give the following example: We all know there is fire in wood. That is knowledge. But this knowledge is useless if we do not know how to light a fire from the wood and use that fire in cooking food. If we know that, then we are wise.

Wisdom then is something more than knowledge. It has its roots in knowledge all right, but it is something more. If knowledge is the tree, wisdom is the fruit. We may have knowledge and yet make mistakes about the fundamental things of life. On the other hand, wise people may not have much knowledge, but they are sound in their judgement and they seldom make mistakes. There are scholars who are unscrupulous and can do anything for selfish reasons. Is scholarship good if it is used to hurt others ?

Knowledge is power. But is it a power for good or for evil ? Often it is for evil. Look at the aborigines all over the world. They are innocent people, though shy and ignorant by our standards. But how they have been exploited over the centuries! They are now on the verge of extinction, or they are preserved only as show-pieces. What a price they have had to pay, and are still paying, for our so-called civilization! The history of civilization is the history of the exploitation of the weak by the strong— of innocent people. The nations who lead the world today are powerful, ruthless, and unscrupulous. They do not worry about the means. By hook or by crook they get what they want. And they are not ashamed of the ways and means they employ.

The rise of colonial powers makes an interesting study. Greed combined with enterprise and superior knowledge of the military art made some nations go round the world looking for loot. They robbed one nation after another, taking advantage of their weakness. Some of those victimized countries were superior in many ways, but they were not strong enough to meet the onslaught of the marauding nations. Often the marauding nations came with the apparent intention of trading, but their real intention was to annex those countries. Then, having once captured power, they treated the people as slaves.

This is what happens when knowledge is divorced from wisdom. It makes us arrogant, unscrupulous, and aggressive. We exploit the weak, and gain what we want by any means possible. We are rash and thoughtless in our actions. We have no self-control, so we are carried away by our passions, bringing more harm to ourselves than good.

A wise person, on the other hand, is thoughtful and never does anything without giving due thought to the consequences. He has full control over himself. He is conscientious and never hurts anybody except under extreme provocation. And if he has to hurt, he hurts with moderation and great sympathy. His knowledge of things may be limited, but he uses that knowledge only for the good of others and never for their harm. The difference between knowledge and wisdom then is that while knowledge means merely having something, wisdom means having something and putting it to good use.

MOTHER EXTRAORDINARY

She was an ordinary woman. There was nothing about her to suggest that she was extraordinary. The same applies to her husband. But Sri Ramakrishna was an unprecedented religious character in history. Sarada Devi, on the other hand, was apparently only a housewife, a good housewife with good human qualities—that's all. But let us see!

Once Sarada Devi was visiting Rameswaram where she was staying as a guest at the palace of the Prince of Ramnad. The Prince, a great admirer of Swami Vivekananda, took special care of Mother, because to him she was like the Swami's guru. One day he directed the Dewan to show Mother and her companions his family's collection of jewellery, and to request Mother to accept, as a token of his respect, any of the jewellery she liked. When Mother came to where the collection lay, the Dewan conveyed the Prince's request to Mother. Mother emphatically declined. The Dewan, a shrewd man, had noticed that with Mother there was a small girl who was Mother's favourite, her niece Radhu. Mother had taken over her care because she had lost her father, and her mother was insane. The Dewan then asked Radhu to choose anything she liked. Alarmed, Mother mentally prayed to Sri Ramakrishna to save her from the embarrassment of Radhu taking one of the priceless jewels spread out before her. But to Mother's great relief, the girl said that she had no use for those things, what she needed was a pencil.

This shows what Mother was like.

A group of people were going to Calcutta for a holy bath in the Ganges and Mother joined the party because she had not seen Sri Ramakrishna for a long time. The older people in the party told everybody to walk fast, so that they could pass through Telo-bhelo before nightfall. Telo-bhelo was a vast open space where robbers ambushed passers-by and robbed them, sometimes even killing them.

As the party proceeded Mother found herself falling behind again and again. She could not walk fast, for her feet were swollen. The other people in the party began to scold Mother, and finally they told her that they could not wait for her and risk being robbed. They advised her to walk faster and catch up with them.

Mother was now alone on the road. When the sun had set and it was getting dark, she came to a place that looked like Telo-bhelo. Suddenly she noticed a figure coming from the opposite direction. It turned out to be a tall black man carrying a big stick in his hand. Mother froze with fear. The man shouted at her, 'Who is there?' in a harsh and threatening voice. Mother then noticed that there was a woman with him. She hurried to her and taking hold of her hands, said, 'Mother, I am your daughter, Sarada. I am going to meet your son-in-law at Dakshineswar. My companions have left me behind. How lucky you two have arrived at this moment!'

The rest of the story is well known. The saint of Dakshineswar later received the couple with due respect, and their relationship remained deep and intimate to the last day.

What did the bandit-couple see in their adopted daughter? Anything extraordinary to explain their extraordinary behaviour?

VEDANTA

Is Vedanta a religion or a philosophy? If we examine Vedanta closely, we will see it is both. As a religion, it tells you how you can reach the goal of your life. As a philosophy, it tells you what that goal is.

What is the goal of our life according to Vedanta? The goal of our life is to become aware of our identity. If we know who or what we are, we are then free. As of now, we feel we are not free. We want many things which we think are legitimately ours, but we never get them. For instance, we do not want to die, but death is inevitable. Why should it be inevitable? Why should we die against our wish? Not only death, but also disease, old age, poverty, bereavement, and so on. Why do these things haunt us all the time? They haunt everyone of us. Why should they? Who is responsible for this mischief?

Look at the other side of the picture: Why should we run after money, power, name and fame, a long life, happiness, pleasure, and so on? Who or what makes us behave like that? The irony is that even if we get them, we are not happy because we do not get as much as we want. Also they do not last long. Having had them, if we begin to lose them, that is heart-breaking. We are caught in a vicious circle: Either we have nothing, or if we have anything, we lose it.

This is what is called bondage. It is as if there is no way of getting out of this situation. Everyone seems to be subject to this.

The *Mundaka Upanishad* talks of two birds on the

same tree. The birds look exactly the same. But they are opposite in nature. One is tasting the fruit of the tree. If the fruit is good, she is very pleased. If it is sour, she is very disappointed. This bird is always swinging between pleasure and pain. We mortals are like this bird, sometimes happy and sometimes unhappy. Vedanta points this out and asks us to look at the other bird. The other bird never tastes the fruit. She simply looks on and is always happy. She does not need anything; she feels she has everything she wants.

According to Vedanta philosophy, the second bird represents the goal of life. When can you be as quiet and peaceful as the second bird? You attain this state when you know your identity. If you know you are supreme, you are free from fear. You also know that you are one without a second, you are everywhere and in everything, you are all.

As a religion, Vedanta tells you what you have to do to reach the goal. Give up your attachment to ephemeral things. Always look for things that never perish. What are those things? Truth, knowledge and bliss. Where are they? All within yourself. Meditate on your real identity as Pure Consciousness. You were never born, and you will never die. Nothing can hurt you. You were always free, always independent, always self-sufficient. Your Self is the Self of all. You are all-pervasive, almighty, and all-knowing. You are self-luminous. You are what you think you are. You are one without a second. You are supreme.

This is the Vedanta religion and this is also the Vedanta philosophy.

FROM THE ABSOLUTE TO THE RELATIVE

Ramakrishna is an example of what the Absolute is, what the Relative is, and how they are related to each other.

As the Absolute, Ramakrishna is nothing and yet everything, nowhere and yet everywhere. He is an atom, and he is also the cosmos. He is inside and outside everything. He is beyond thought, beyond speech. There is no way of describing the Absolute.

But does the Absolute exist anywhere except in imagination? Is it a state of mind? Or, better, a state of mindlessness? The matter is debatable. Perhaps the Absolute is only an assumption. If it is an assumption, how can it be identified with a human being? How can Ramakrishna be an Absolute? Is the Absolute one, or can there be many Absolutes?

Perhaps the best or the only thing one can say about the Absolute is that it is the Absolute. To say anything else about it is meaningless. To say that Ramakrishna was the Absolute or an Absolute hardly makes any sense. When the word 'Absolute' is not clear, what purpose does it serve in applying it to Ramakrishna? What particular development in Ramakrishna calls for the use of this description? No doubt Ramakrishna was an extraordinary person. But in what sense was he the Absolute?

The Absolute is the extreme. It is the highest point, the summit. But of what? It does not matter of what. The Absolute is a point where all opposites meet. It is the Absolute which gives the Relative a semblance of reality. It is the support of everything else.

What is meant when it is said that Ramakrishna is the Absolute? It means that Ramakrishna has reached a point beyond which there is nothing. Ramakrishna often referred to this as the roof of a building, its highest point. Ramakrishna himself mentions what happens when you reach this point. You are silent. You are silent because there is nothing to talk about; all diversity having been wiped out, there is only Oneness. The Oneness is all-embracing; the seer, the seen, and the seeing—all these are telescoped into one. You are in *samadhi*, the ecstasy which makes you feel one with everything; you lose yourself in your Self. This is when you are the Absolute.

Ramakrishna was the Absolute, he was also the Relative. From the Absolute to the Relative, and then again back to the Absolute—this is how he lived. He described this as climbing up to the roof and coming down again. From One to Many, and from Many to One—this is how he lived his life. When he was One, he was in *Nirvikalpa Samadhi,* a state one can say nothing about. But he did not stay there too long a time, though it was a blissful state. His heart was with the Many. He hurried back from that bliss to the Relative state to share the pleasure and pain of the many. His roots were in the Absolute, in the One, in the bliss of the Self, but he preferred to be in the Relative, with the Many, sharing the pleasure and pain of all. He loved to be one of the Many.

The Absolute and the Relative are one and the same. The difference is only in the angle from which you look at it. Ramakrishna was both the Absolute and the Relative. He was the Absolute when he enfolded the whole world within himself, and he was the Relative when he spread himself out, entering everything.

COOPERATION AND COMPETITION

How good life would be if we, individuals and nations, could cooperate with one another! Not that we do not cooperate. We do, but not to the extent we ought to. The progress civilization has made is the outcome of the collective efforts of mankind as a whole. Different nations have made their contributions, some more and some less, some more in science and technology, some more in arts and literature; even the so-called backward countries have made substantial contributions in one field or another, and those contributions have been recognized and are now highly appreciated. Sometimes the recognition of a country's contribution comes late, but happily it does come. An outstanding person may be born in a country—a poet, a scientist, a sportsman, a philosopher or an artist. The country itself, perhaps in Africa, may not be enlightened, yet a genius comes from there out of the blue and the world is taken aback by his performance. What that genius gives to the world may be something people remember for generations together. It may be a poem, a machine, a way of doing things, a picture, a theory, an interpretation of a scientific phenomenon, and so on. It may mark the turning-point of a whole system of philosophical thinking, or even of human relationship.

'Give-and-take' is the law of life. An individual has to do all he can for his community and for the country to which he belongs. In so doing he attains his fulfilment. This applies not only to individuals, but also to communities and countries. The world is nowadays referred to as 'a global village'. It is big in size, still it is a village in the sense that we have to have good neighbourly relations with one another. Good or bad, whatever comes we have to share it with one another. We cannot live in isolation. If there is a calamity, we will fight it together. If oil has been struck somewhere, it is a good fortune which we will share together. If one of us in this global village has turned out to be a good sportsman, a poet, a scientist, an engineer, or a musician, we are all proud of him. The principle is that we are all one.

If one person cooperates with another, it is not that the former is doing a favour to the latter. They are only helping each other and they are doing so for mutual benefit only. But what is wrong if they compete with each other in being good and doing good? If two scientists compete with each other in solving a scientific problem, there can be nothing wrong there provided their discovery is for the common benefit of the whole world. If a scientist discovers a drug for the cure of cancer, that is a great service to humanity. In fact, all over the world institutions and individuals are trying to discover a drug for cancer. They may be competing with one another in this. There is nothing wrong in this so long as it is for the good of humanity as a whole. Maybe they will earn some money this way. They are welcome to do so since they are earning money in return for the great service they are rendering to mankind.

Cooperation and competition, both may be good or bad depending upon the purpose behind them. A band of robbers working together may make great sacrifices for each other, but whatever they do is for selfish gain and the methods they adopt are also bad. Cooperation and competition, both can be good, if the ends and the means adopted are good.

NATIONAL INTEGRATION

There are people who question if India can be called a 'nation' in the sense the word is understood. Perhaps not. Politically India has never been one country except during the reigns of Asoka and Akbar in the early days and during the British rule in recent times. It has been a country divided into small and large states, each of them distinct in terms of language, and in some cases, even in terms of race. There have also been sporadic clashes between one state and another, but, by and large, they have maintained good neighbourly relations with each other. Sometimes they clashed, but they never had a prolonged war. Their dispute might have been over boundaries, or over a matter of hurt prestige. Usually they settled the dispute amicably, often through matrimony.

The history of India is a history of peaceful co-existence. No one can tell how many races came from outside, when they came, from where, and why. Presumably, they left their homeland because of some natural calamity, war, or persecution by other races. Perhaps they had no choice. They had heard of India, its wealth, and its peace-loving people. When they arrived, no one tried to stop them at the border. In fact, India had always maintained an open-border policy, so that those people had no difficulty entering the country and finding a place to stay. They stayed wherever they found an open space and the people around friendly and hospitable. Naturally they preferred a place nearest to their erstwhile homeland in terms of climate and other living conditions. Those who had lived in hills and forests naturally set up their new home there, for they lived by hunting and India had plenty of hills and forests rich with game in those days. There were others who were basically agriculturists and craftsmen. Perhaps they brought new techniques with them, which India welcomed, and they too had no difficulty finding a place to stay. This process went on over the centuries. The present population of India represents a wide spectrum of racial characteristics, which is evidence of this immigration. India has, however, proved a good melting-pot: There has been such an admixture of blood that it is now difficult to identify the races that came from outside. The admixture has been complete even at the linguistic and religious levels, so that vast chunks of people have now a common language and a common religious belief. This unification is voluntary, and is the outcome of mutual acceptance.

Long ago, Indian rishis conceived the idea of 'Unity in Diversity'. They realized that diversity was natural and inevitable. Any attempt to smother it would be fatal. The rule that governs the relations between the diverse groups and communities should be one of love and good will. 'Live and let live', this should be the motto. On the surface, India looks divided but underneath there is the sense of oneness which keeps its diverse communities together; this is the kind of unity which India possesses. At the root of this unity is mutual love and respect.

Real national integration is possible only on the basis of this love and respect. No legislation, or paper agreement can sustain the unity of a nation. Only love can.

TRUTH AND SILENCE

The word *muni* is common to both Hindu and Buddhist traditions, but its connotation is not the same to them. The Hindu tradition takes the word to mean one who has conquered his mind and has, in consequence, attained Self-Knowledge and realized Truth. To a Buddhist the word, however, means one who is 'silent', or 'mute'. Why is he silent? He is silent because it is part of his asceticism. Why should he talk? What is there to talk about? And to whom would he talk? Is it not waste of time and energy talking to others? Buddha is often referred to as 'Shakya Muni', the mute one of the Shakya clan. This was because Buddha often gave evasive replies if people asked him about God or the Self. To this day people do not know exactly what Buddha's stand was on God or the Self or the Ultimate Reality. Some people say 'silence' had to be his answer, for what he had to say was beyond thought and speech.

Buddha did not like to see people arguing about metaphysics. He thought it was waste of time. But the irony is that just because of or in spite of this attitude towards philosophy, much philosophy has grown and is still growing, centering round Buddha. Crucial to Buddha's teachings is *nirvana,* which he describes as the goal of life. But what is *nirvana* ? The debate about its meaning is still going on. One school of thought explains *nirvana* as going out, extinction, or dissolution. The meaning is negative. Another school holds that *nirvana* has an affirmative meaning. It means infinite bliss. Whether it is extinction or infinite bliss, it hardly means anything to an ordinary person. Buddha's silence is understandable under the circumstances.

It is interesting to note that the Hindu tradition is not exactly silent, but admits that the nature of the Ultimate Reality, known also as Truth or the Self or Brahman, cannot be described. It is beyond thought and speech. Again and again the Upanishads say that the subject cannot be an object, it cannot be known like other things are known. Truth is self-evident. It is like a lamp which does not need a second lamp to reveal itself. Truth is the ground of everything. It is universal and eternal. It is the self of everybody and everything. It is existence itself. It is both immanent and transcendent. It is knowledge and it is also bliss. It is without beginning and without end. It is infinite. It is everything.

While admitting that Truth is beyond thought and speech, the Hindu tradition still insists that the search for Truth must be man's preoccupation in life. There are people who have sought and finally found Truth. They are not charlatans; their life and character bear testimony to their great wisdom. A genuine seeker of Truth goes to such a person and begs to be taught. The teacher is not silent, he takes great pains to explain Truth to him. He knows it is difficult, yet he tries. He himself is an exposition of Truth and the disciple learns about Truth, just from being with the teacher. Finally he also realizes Truth. It is like a lamp being lit by another. Both Hinduism and Buddhism have the same goal and almost the same methods of self-discipline. If they have any difference, their difference is semantic. Truth is the goal, and when you reach that goal, you are overwhelmed with joy. All your organs go within, and your response to the world around is through silence.

LEADERSHIP

A leader is one who is utterly selfless. He does not think of his own comfort, he only thinks of how best he can serve others. He does not want any power, but power comes to him in spite of himself. People love him because they know he loves them and he loves them more than they love him. They know he is ready to make any sacrifice necessary for their sake. He does not talk of what he has done for them in the past and what he is going to do in the future. He is silent about his work. His work speaks for him. He deems it a privilege to be able to serve others. He expects nothing in return. He serves because he loves to serve. He does not want money, power, or praise for what he is doing. He is happy if what he is doing proves beneficial to the people. He is modest and always conscious of his limitations. He can only do his best, and he is happy if what he has done is of any use to the people.

A good leader always means well, but that is not to say that he will do something immoral or something apparently good but not really good. He will even risk doing something unpopular if it is necessary in the larger interests of the people. No doubt the well-being of his people is his first priority, but he will not do anything unethical. People may be disappointed, even offended, but he will not compromise his principles. To him the means are as important as the ends. National interests are surely of the highest value to him, but he does not believe that moral principles can be sacrificed for their sake. A dishonest man can never lead his people to a good future. When people know he is dishonest, they will have no respect for him and will not trust him. If the nation is in a crisis, they will hardly have any faith in his leadership. An unscrupulous man is basically a weak man; he is a coward. He will betray his country at the first hint of any personal insecurity.

A leader must be a man of great moral strength. He may be exposed to temptations, but he will never succumb. Not only his own people, but the people of other countries also must respect him, first as a man and then, as a leader. He must be honest, straightforward, and frank. International relations must be based on universally accepted moral principles. It is for the leaders to uphold these principles in their personal life as well as in their dealings with other nations. 'Truth must prevail.' In no circumstances should truth be sacrificed. Like truth, principles such as justice, charity, and equality should be upheld. Goodwill, friendship, and mutual trust should be promoted. There can be no peace if diplomacy is characterized by secrecy and unscrupulousness. Leaders should take the lead in these matters. Real leaders are world leaders. They are people who take the world as one and mankind as a single family. They are as much concerned with the well-being of other nations as of the nation they lead. They know there can be no peace and no prosperity which are not shared by all.

A true leader leads more morally than politically. His message is more in his personal life and character than in his public pronouncements. He is concerned not only with the immediate, but also with the future. He is the epitome of the best in man.

THE MESSAGE OF THE UPANISHADS

The message of all the Upanishads is the same: Self-knowledge. But they differ in the emphasis they give to different aspects of that message. For instance, the *Isha Upanishad* says there is a veil covering the Truth. That veil is so dazzling that we are not able to see what is behind it. It is a warning lest we be carried away by the appearance of things.

The *Katha Upanishad* also sounds a note of warning about thinking that we know everything. The ignorant are compared to blind people going about without knowing where they are going. And they are so vain that they are not able to see their own folly.

According to the *Mundaka Upanishad*, ignorance is like a knot that we have to untie. Because of this knot we are not able to reach the Self in our heart. We have to get rid of this knot by any means.

The *Chhandogya Upanishad* reminds us that knowledge is power and ignorance is weakness. Knowledge means Self-knowledge. The *Chhandogya* also tells us that Brahman alone is real and everything else is merely a name, a word.

According to the *Brihadaranyaka Upanishad*, unreality is darkness, a kind of death. The *Brihadaranyaka* also defines *maya* as a mere semblance, an appearance.

The *Prashna Upanishad* says that the barrier between us and Brahman is our own ignorance. And because of our ignorance we tend to be crooked, dishonest, and foolish.

The *Shvetashvatara Upanishad* defines God as a *mayin*, a magician. He casts a spell on us, and as a result, we take sense pleasures to be real and run after them. Instead of trying to realize the Truth, which is the goal of life, we remain enmeshed in the delusions of life. Like other Upanishads, the *Shvetashvatara* also preaches non-dualism, but it is not fanatical about this. It seems to concede that there are also other ways of reaching the goal. Some verses are clearly dualistic. Shankara takes great pains in trying to establish non-dualism in his commentary on this Upanishad, but it is doubtful if he succeeds.

In a nutshell, the Upanishads tell us that Brahman alone is real, and the phenomenal world we live in and deal with is not real. It is like a shadow. But there is no shadow unless there is something real. The world exists because Brahman exists. The goal of life is to realize this and to realize also that the inmost being—that is, the Self in every thing and in every being—is this Brahman.

Brahman is both *saguna*, with qualities (or, *apara*, lower), and *nirguna*, without qualities (or, *para*, higher). Saguna Brahman is Ishvara, the Lord of the universe. Nirguna Brahman is the Absolute. Saguna Brahman is personal. Nirguna Brahman is impersonal. Saguna Brahman includes both living and non-living objects. Nirguna Brahman is Existence Absolute, Consciousness Absolute, Bliss Absolute (*Sat + Chit + Ananda*). All that exists is a manifestation of Nirguna Brahman. It is the Truth of all truths, the Reality of all realities. At this point there is only one, and therefore there is no fear. All categories fade in Nirguna Brahman. It is like rivers merging into the sea. They no longer have an identity of their own.

To know Brahman is to be Brahman. This is liberation.

SWAMI AKHANDANANDA

Almost everybody called Swami Akhandananda 'Baba' because he had raised many orphans. The orphans called him 'Baba' and his admirers also did the same. His brother-disciples called him 'Ganga', a shortened form of 'Gangadhar', his pre-monastic name. Swami Vivekananda, however, called him 'Ganges', the English name of the river.

All the disciples of Sri Ramakrishna were unique, each in his own way. Swami Akhandananda was no exception. He was born a brahmin, and even when he was a mere boy, he practised extreme austerities. He ate only one meal a day and he himself cooked it. He also bathed thrice in the Ganges everyday. He had other habits which verged on idiosyncrasies.

He was still very young when he came to Sri Ramakrishna. The Master pointed out to him the priorities in spiritual life and asked him to stick to them. He advised him to follow Swami Vivekananda, which he did. The two brother-monks remained close to each other to the end.

Soon after the Master's passing away, the disciples scattered wherever they could in search of God. The Himalayas always attracted Swami Akhandananda, and there he went and disappeared. For years no one knew where he was, he was even taken for dead. Finally he was discovered at Almora in the company of Tibetan monks. He had gone into Tibet, courted the monks and lived there as one of them. Swami Akhandananda later held his audience spellbound when he narrated his Tibetan experiences.

Though he stayed a while with his brother-disciples,

the Himalayas called him again. This time he decided he would walk along the Ganges till he reached them. He had gone up to Murshidabad when a sight brought him to a halt: A little girl crying loudly. When he asked her why she was crying, she said her mother had sent her to fetch some water and she had come to the market-place with their only earthen pitcher. She filled it with water from the tubewell and was carrying it back when it slipped from her hands and broke into pieces. She knew her mother had no money to buy another pitcher and would beat her when she went back home.

Swami Akhandananda was moved. He himself had very little money, yet he gave her a few coins to buy a new pitcher. Some children saw the Swami hand the money to the girl and at once surrounded him and begged for money to buy something to eat. The Swami soon discovered a famine was raging there and decided to leave the place immediately, for he felt it would be a crime to stay there and be a burden on the people when they themselves were starving.

Just as he was leaving, he heard there was an old woman dying of cholera and had no one to look after her. He rushed to her cottage and started nursing her. He washed and took care of her day and night. When the woman recovered she said to him, 'You must have been my son in my previous life.' He affectionately replied, 'I am your son even in this life.'

VALUES IN MODERN LIFE

In a discussion of values, possibly we will not agree with one another. What is a value, for instance? The dictionary meaning of the word is anything we think of as important—anything that we think highly of. It may be health, wealth, political power or social standing, and so on. Each individual has his own values—not just one value; probably many values and those too ever-changing. Sweets were my highest value as a child. As I grew older and started going to school, I began to say, 'When am I going to beat the top boy in the class?' My values changed as I was growing.

The Hindu scriptures say that life has a twofold purpose, one *abhyudaya* and the other *nihshreyasa*. *Abhyudaya* means rising higher, higher and higher in physical, material and intellectual terms all the time. The spirit of *abhyudaya* impels you not to stay stuck where you are. You never say, 'Oh, I have had enough, I don't need to go further.' You always go on and on and on. Life is a struggle. If you sit back and say, 'Oh, I have had enough. Let me rest now,' that is as good as death. 'No—I will not be contented.'

Christian Theology says that in each one of us there is something called 'divine discontent'. It urges us to go forward, to know more, to achieve higher and higher things. Sometimes we are content with some physical comfort; but very soon we begin to say, 'No, this is not enough, there are other things I would like to have.' Finally, as you rise higher and higher, you reach a point when you feel 'I have everything, I have achieved everything I wanted to. And yet I am not happy.' You have come to the state of seeking *nihshreyasa*, the highest, described in Hindu Philosophy as Self-realization or God-realization.

Thus we move from lower values to higher values. At first your values centre round good food, good clothing, good housing, physical well-being, etc. But soon you acquire higher and finer values such as reading a good book, visiting a picture gallery or reading some good poetry or good fiction. You thus move slowly from the gross to the fine. The dog may be a clever animal, but it is happy if it has enough to eat and if his master sometimes pats him on the back. That's all. But man is never content with gross values. He is a special animal, he is next to God. He is never, never satisfied. This discontent is a blessing, as it urges you to reach the highest—God-realization, attainment of Godhood, or becoming a perfect man. The Bible says: 'Be thou perfect as thy Father in heaven is perfect.' A perfect man never admits he is perfect. He may be perfect in the eyes of his friends. Everybody may point to him and say, 'Here is a perfect man.' 'Far from it, No, No,' he will say. He will not admit that he is perfect. No. He will say that he has further to go, 'miles to go,' as the poet says. 'I want to go on and on,' he says.

So, we are always moving from lower to higher values. We keep moving all the time. Our sights are always going up and up.

What is the Indian attitude towards values? We never stop. I want something; when I get that, I want something higher, something better. That is the Indian attitude towards values. At last we want the highest—God- or Self-realization.

DESTINY

What role does destiny play in our life? Some people say destiny is supreme. If anything good happens to you, it is because of your destiny. The same is the case if something bad happens. In fact, everything is pre-determined. Whatever happens is the result of your past. There is the law of cause and effect operating in Nature and also in human life. It is the cause that becomes the effect. The seed is the tree. 'Something out of nothing' is an absurd idea. There is always a cause behind an effect, and destiny is the law which makes this possible.

But can a good cause produce a bad effect, or a bad cause produce a good effect? More to the point, if destiny is a law, it is to be expected that it will be infallible. In our day-to-day life, we see paradoxes for which there is no explanation. For instance, we see an honest man starving while a dishonest man is rolling in wealth. If destiny is a law, it should not let this happen. It should punish dishonesty and reward honesty. In practice, we, however, see just the reverse, which means that destiny works like the whim of a powerful potentate.

Often religious people describe God as a whimsical potentate. They say whatever happens is not according to a law framed by a sensible person; it is the whim of a dictator mad with power. Stupid people kowtow to him, hoping they will be able to win his favour. They may do a wrong, but if they are able to please him, they will escape punishment. Similarly, if they need something out of their reach, they hope they will be able to get it by flattering this whimsical person.

Indeed, the word *destiny* is a riddle. If it is defined as a principle of cause and effect, the principle then is not a rational one. It is something like madness. If God is responsible for all that happens in the world, we have then more reasons to fear Him than to love Him.

There is one school of thought which does not blame or praise God for anything. God is the source of the power that makes things happen, but He Himself does nothing. Those who use that power are responsible. The lamp is not responsible if its light is used to forge a document. Those who forge the document are responsible.

This school of thought also holds that man is responsible for what he now is and what he is going to be in the future. He is the maker of his own destiny. This school advocates that man should work for others and not for himself. In fact, he should work for work's sake. He should feel happy if others are happy and feel unhappy if others are unhappy. He does not need to acknowledge anything such as destiny outside of himself. He is his own master.

But is there no such thing as God or destiny? God certainly exists and also perhaps destiny. God oversees things so that a good man is rightly rewarded and a bad man punished in proportion to the bad things he has done. But what about those instances in which a good man is punished without any rhyme or reason, whereas a bad man gets away with the bad things he has done? There is really no explanation for this. It may be argued that the good man is being punished for the bad things he did in a previous life. Now the question arises if there is such a thing as reincarnation. Recent enquiries confirm that reincarnation is a reality, and man carries over from one life to another the results of his actions.

SPIRITUALITY

Karl Marx once described religion as the 'opium' of the masses. But very few people know Marx also said that religion is the 'only heart in a heartless world'. Think of it—the only heart! What does heart stand for? Love, kindness, compassion.

In fact Love is God and God is Love. Similarly, all religions say religion is love and love is religion. Karl Marx denied religion. Yet he also says that if there is any heart anywhere, it is only in the religious people. This is what practical spirituality is.

Swami Vivekananda says: Love everybody, even a criminal, even one whom you consider your enemy. When you love one, you are indeed loving yourself. All holy men, saints and sages, irrespective of religious denominations or country or community, have this love. Love has to be universal. Everyone loves his own friends or children. But that is not true love; true love makes no distinction. It is love for all. There is no 'why' in this love. I love because, as Swami Vivekananda says, 'I love to love.'

There was once a war in Kashmir between the Muslims and the Sikhs. As the war went on, drinking water gradually became very scarce. One evening the Sikh soldiers were resting after a day's fight. They were tired and very thirsty because they had no time to drink water while fighting. Moreover where was water to be found? There was none anywhere in the hills. They kept searching and after a long while, they were able to collect some water. The Sikh Guru was watching everything. He knew how thirsty his soldiers were. Yet he said, 'First serve water to the Muslims and then we will drink.'

Practical spirituality is this kind of concern for everybody. Most people are concerned for their own children. But that is nothing. That is only natural. But if you are concerned for every child, no matter who that child is, that is genuine love.

Before going to the West, Swami Vivekananda led the life of a wandering monk. One day he met Swami Turiyananda, one of his brother-disciples, somewhere. They eagerly conversed, exchanging news. Swami Vivekananda at last told his brother-disciple, 'Brother, I don't know whether I have realized God or not. But I feel my heart has become vast. I now feel for everybody.' This feeling, this concern for everybody, is the climax that you reach in your religious endeavour. Honesty and love are the two criteria of religion. And when you meet an individual, honest and concerned about the welfare of others, you know he is really spiritual.

We need this kind of religion. Religion is realization and realization requires practice. We have to develop a feeling that we will never compromise where the question of truth is involved. Think of Kshudiram, Sri Ramakrishna's father. He was a poor village brahmin. Once a rich man wanted him to give false evidence in court for he was highly respected. People knew he was a man who would never tell a lie. If he went to the court and gave false evidence for that rich man, the latter would win the case. Kshudiram, however, refused to oblige. This angered the rich man who now started a number of false suits against him. As a result Kshudiram had to leave the village without one penny. But all the same, he was happy. He was happy because he had not succumbed to fear. He had remained firm in his devotion to Truth.

Marx was right. Religion is the only heart in a heartless world, for it is religion and religion only that makes you love the whole world and sacrifice everything for the sake of Truth.

MODESTY

There are people who love to use 'I' as often as possible; there are also people who avoid using it altogether, if they can. If the conclusion is drawn that the first group of people are all vain and the second group are all modest, will it be correct? Doubtful. What if the modesty of the second group is only a make-believe? They may be vain and haughty, but they pretend otherwise, perhaps for some mischievous purpose. Will you call them modest? They may be trying to fool you. How can you trust them?

There is nothing wrong in using 'I', provided you use it without any desire to impress others. If you are simply making a statement of fact, there can be nothing wrong in your repeating 'I'. Suppose you are warning others about bad habits like smoking and you mention how those habits have hurt you and in that connection you use the pronoun 'I' again and again, can that be treated as vanity? It will be unfair to call it vanity; more likely it is self-deprecation, and that is equally bad. Self-deprecation may be vanity in disguise; by no means can it be called modesty.

Real modesty is recognition of one's distance from one's goals. If you recognize that you have far to go to reach your goals, you are modest. You do not then talk of what you have achieved; maybe you will then talk of what you have yet to achieve. Modesty comes when you learn to admire others for what they have achieved and come to recognize how far behind you are compared with them. It is not that you are jealous of them; you only hope that you may also someday reach where they are already. Not only that, you try to learn from them whatever good qualities they have.

Modesty is constant self-assessment. It is not finding fault with yourself just as it is not closing your eyes to your shortcomings. It is constantly reminding yourself of your goals and urging yourself to go faster than you are now going. You do not lose heart that you have not yet reached the peak; you only keep hoping that since others have reached the peak you will also reach it someday. You say to yourself that you will not only reach the peak, you will reach a higher place if there is one. You will always keep pushing forward.

Modesty is a kind of digging and exploring, a ceaseless process which never tires you but encourages you to go deeper and deeper within yourself. As you go deeper, you are amazed at what you discover. You no longer feel like talking about yourself. You are then driven by your curiosity to have a closer look at yourself than you have so far had. You are, in fact, amazed that there is so much wealth lying within yourself, but you never want to talk about it. You only want to dig and explore deeper. You have no time to talk about it. Another name for modesty is introspection. You watch and study yourself. You take note of everything you have within yourself: good and bad. You are not content with yourself. You are happy if you are progressing, but you will be happier if you can progress faster. Watch every thought you think, every word you say, and everything you do. You have to be answerable to yourself for what you do or what you are. You are modest when you learn to judge yourself impartially.

MOTHER

Sarada Devi once asked Sri Ramakrishna, 'Who am I to you?' Sri Ramakrishna promptly replied, 'You are my mother.' As if to make it more explicit, he added that she was the mother who gave birth to him, the mother who was in the temple, and the mother now talking to him, all rolled into one.

Once Hriday asked Mother how she looked upon Sri Ramakrishna. She replied he was at once her son, father, teacher and husband, he was everything. What is important is that she meant what she said.

Mother used to say that she was mother to all, good or bad. In fact, there used to be a criminal who enjoyed her affection as much as a holy man. Even birds and animals were her children. God as Mother is a well-known Hindu concept. Mother was a living example of that concept. Mother once said, 'The Master has left me behind to teach people to worship God as Mother.' Let us say people loved her as mother, but did they love her as God also? Interestingly, Mother did not like anybody to worship her as God. If anybody did, she would protest. She would prefer being a normal human mother rather than God worshipped as Mother. A monk—Rashbehari was his name—had lost his mother at birth. He never called any woman 'mother', as if in protest. He lived with Mother and served her like anybody else. While everybody else called Mother 'Mother', he did not. He, however, respected her in a way that verged on worship. Mother observed his behaviour. One day she called him and asked him to go and call a certain young man. She said, 'Go and say "Mother is calling you." ' The young man said, 'Yes, I'll say that you are calling, but I will not say "Mother" is calling.' Mother asked, 'Why not?' Mother was not satisfied, she asked him to repeat what exactly he was going to say. Rashbehari said what he was going to say, but omitted the word 'Mother'. But she was firm and made it clear that she wanted him to use her exact words.

At last, Rashbehari came out with his secret. He said he had never addressed his own mother as mother, for she died at his birth. Mother then firmly said that she was his real mother. 'How do I know that?', Rashbehari asked. Mother replied with great emphasis, 'I am your mother, and that is that. Whether you know it or not is immaterial.'

Rashbehari was taken aback. He was not prepared for such a reply. He still had doubts in his mind. He asked, 'If you are my real mother, why should I then address you the way I do? I always address you with the formal *you*. A son never addresses his mother that way.' Mother calmly said, 'Address me the way a son addresses his mother. You have no reason to be formal.'

This totally changed Rashbehari's dealings with Mother. From then on, Mother was simply mother to him. The change was not a change of his address, it was a change in himself. He was now part and parcel of Mother.

Sri Ramakrishna had told Mother to be a mother to everybody. How did it change those who came in contact with her? It changed them because they felt they were under the care of Mother. This feeling made them think and act like Mother wanted. What can be a more precious reward to a child than a smile from her mother? It was this smile that determined the course of life of those who believed they were Mother's children.

'SIR, HAVE YOU SEEN GOD ?'

Swami Vivekananda once put this question to Sri Ra-makrishna. He had put the same question to others, but the answers he got were evasive. This led him to think that God did not exist. He had read many books by Western thinkers and they had further confirmed his disbe-lief.

But Swami Vivekananda was not the only person of his time who did not believe in God. The whole generation of young people, his contemporaries, did not believe in Him. In fact, they did not believe in religion at all. Most of the educated young people had nothing but contempt for reli-gious beliefs and practices. They claimed to be rational, and they regarded being rational as shunning anything that passed as religion and culture. They imitated the West as best they could and thought everything Western was good and right.

Sri Ramakrishna's reply to Swami Vivekananda was, however, stunning. He said he had not only seen God, but had seen Him as clearly as he was seeing Swami Vive-kananda. And if Swami Vivekananda so wished, he could show God to him too. It is immaterial whether Sri Ra-makrishna could show God to Swami Vivekananda or not. The conviction with which Sri Ramakrishna said this *is* material. Obviously Sri Ramakrishna meant that he him-self was a man, seeing whom people could know what God was like. It was not his physical appearance, but his character that showed how and where God differed from man. According to Hindu philosophy, a man who knows God is so transformed that he becomes like God Himself. When you look at such a person, you know you are look-

ing at God. Sri Ramakrishna did not assert that he was
God; his character convinced many people that he was
God. Whether he was God or not, he was certainly a
Godlike person.

As days passed, Swami Vivekananda began to understand Sri Ramakrishna. He began to see God in him
more and more. He had read books about God and God-
men, but it was not the same as seeing Sri Ramakrishna.
Seeing Sri Ramakrishna was like being God yourself. It
was becoming aware of the awakening of a new power
within yourself. You felt you were not the same person
as before.

Swami Vivekananda did not want India to imitate the
West. He wanted it to be a better India. He realized that
times had changed and were still changing. No country
could always remain the same. If it remained the same, it
meant it was dead. It must change, but basically it must remain the same so far as its roots are concerned—its values,
traditions, aims of life.

But what has a country's progress got to do with God?
If a country decides to leave its future in the hands of God,
it is doomed. India has never been fatalistic that way. Being religious does not mean surrendering one's fate to an
unknown power called 'God'. It means, first and foremost,
honesty and hard work. A truly religious man is as careful
about the ends he chooses as about the means he uses in
attaining them. India has always attached as much importance to the means as to the ends. Religion has no meaning
if the ends and means do not correspond.

If seeing God means becoming God, the question
Swami Vivekananda put to Sri Ramakrishna and the answer he received have a meaning which every country and
every individual should bear in mind.

BUDDHISM AND VEDANTA

It is wrong to think that Buddhism and Vedanta have two opposite viewpoints. They are very much alike, if not the same. The difference, if any at all, is in details, and in nomenclature.

Much of what Buddha teaches comes from the Upanishads. Buddha, however, does not acknowledge this; he, in fact, does not acknowledge his indebtedness to any book or teacher. That is one reason why he is sometimes described as an 'atheist'. If somebody came and asked him, 'Sir, is there a God?' Buddha would say, 'Have I ever told you that there is a God?' The man might then say, 'Does that mean there is no God?' Buddha's reply would then be, 'Have I ever said that there is no God?'

He spoke thus because he was against idle talk about religion. To him religion was realization.

There is, however, the question how you can reconcile Buddha's theory of 'no-soul', *Anatma*, with the conviction of Vedanta that there is a permanent Self. True, Buddha laid great stress on *Nairatmavada* (the theory of no-self) while Vedanta lays stress on the existence of the Atman (the Self). But there is a difference between the self of Buddha and the Self of Vedanta. Buddha's self is the individual self of Vedanta, a product of Avidya; for both it is empirically real, otherwise it is unreal.

The Upanishads speak of Atman as Reality. To Buddha this Reality was Bodhi. He did not, however, say that Bodhi was Atman. To him Atman was Jiva and they were both unreal. Thus the difference between Buddhism and Vedanta is mainly a matter of nomenclature.

The question of the difference between Buddha's *nirvana* and Vedanta's *mukti* is also largely a matter of words. There is actually little or no difference in the two.

Buddha always harped on suffering. He saw suffering everywhere, in every being. How do you overcome this suffering? By self-control. He advocated self-control for all.

This was not only Buddha's view. This has been the view of all saints and sages. Some people think Buddha was a pessimist. This is not fair. All he has done is to draw our attention to the stark realities of life.

If Buddha was a pessimist, so in that sense is Vedanta and all religious teachings. Religion begins with the query of how to attain lasting happiness. If it does not give one eternal joy, what is it for then?

According to Buddha, *nirvana* is the goal of life. But what is *nirvana* ? It is wrongly understood to mean 'annihilation'. *Nirvana* is freedom, freedom from change. It is unchangeable Reality—a state of eternal peace. There is no way of describing this peace. It is freedom (*mukti*) from the ego, from delusion, from ignorance.

But how do you get this freedom? According to Vedanta, you get this freedom through transcendental knowledge. It is not an intellectual experience, but a state of being, a complete transformation of character. Christ calls it *Perfection*. (John viii 32). Vedanta describes it as the direct, immediate knowledge of the Self, which is *Sat-Chit-Ananda* (Existence-Intelligence-Bliss).

Both Buddhism and Vedanta prefer practice to theory. Buddha said to Ananda, 'Be a lamp unto yourself.' That is, you have to be your own guide; you cannot depend upon others. You yourself have to attain first-hand experience of truth. This is why it is said, 'Religion is realization.'

SWAMI VIVEKANANDA'S HOME-COMING

S wami Vivekananda left India for the USA on 31 May 1893. He was going to Chicago to attend the first ever Parliament of Religions to be held there on 11 September of that year.

He was at first reluctant; however, a group of young men of Madras prevailed upon him to go. He too began to feel that it was his Master's wish that he should do so. He even told a brother-disciple that the Parliament was being held for his sake. At the time the idea seemed absurd, but the later course of events proved that he was right.

The Parliament began on 11 September. His very first speech cast a spell on the audience. But what did he say? He said there was a common truth underlying all religions and pleaded for peace and harmony among them.

His speeches had a tremendous appeal to people everywhere. One newspaper said that sending Christian missionaries to India to preach religion was a sheer waste of money. Other sections of the press said that Americans had better learn religion from India.

When the report of Swami Vivekananda's success appeared in the Indian press, the whole country was overjoyed.

Swamiji spent about four years in the West returning to India via Colombo on 26 January 1897. Thousands of people gathered to see him at every stop of his journey to Calcutta. At one place some one carried a banner with the inscription: 'See the conquering hero comes!'

After visiting a few places in and around Madras Swamiji took a boat for Calcutta, arriving at Budge Budge

on the night of 18 January. The next day, that is, on the
19th, a special train brought him to Calcutta. More than
twenty thousand people received him with shouts of 'Victory to Swami Vivekananda'. The students of Ripon College (now Surendranath College), seated him in a horse-
drawn carriage, removed the horses and pulled the carriage
themselves. They first stopped at their own college where
Swamiji spoke to the students after which they stopped at
Mitra Institution. They then took him to Pasupati Basu's
house. From there Swamiji went to Alambazar Math where
his brother-disciples were waiting for him. A few days after
this he was given a reception by the citizens of Calcutta at
the Shobhabazar Rajbati. Here Swamiji gave a touching
speech describing himself as 'a mere boy of Calcutta'.

One hundred years later

A hundred years have passed since then. The country
is now celebrating the centenary of Swamiji's return. This
return is significant because it marks the beginning of a
new age for India. In the course of his tour through the
country he drew the attention of his countrymen to their
problems and told them what they should do to solve them.
Gandhiji, Rajagopalachari, Sri Aurobindo, Netaji—almost
every patriot acknowledges his indebtedness to Swamiji. If
the country is free today, it is because of the dynamism
Swamiji infused into the nation.

All that took place one hundred years ago when
Swamiji returned—a special train, thousands of people
standing along the tracks, crowds at the railway stations, (a
portrait of) Swamiji inside a horse-carriage, young students
pulling the carriage—the whole drama of his return has
been re-enacted. And celebrations will continue for a
whole year—till February 1998.

SARGACHHI : ONE HUNDRED YEARS LATER

Swami Akhandananda loved to travel. He was barely twenty when he paid his first visit to the Himalayas. He travelled alone most of the time. And of course he hardly ever had any money with him. Strangely enough, this was no problem with him. He did not beg, but people, on their own, gave him whatever he needed. Was it because of his tender age? Partly, but perhaps there were other reasons also. His looks, for instance. His command of Hindi, also. But, more than anything, his monastic qualities must have impressed people. He had a large circle of friends among the monks. These monks belonged to different schools, but each of them accepted him as their own. He was known all over the Himalayas. He knew the Himalayas like the back of his hand. Sometimes he was absent from the Calcutta monastery for years. His brother-disciples even thought he was dead. There was a special reason why they thought this was so. The fact was, he was trying to get into Tibet, and in those days that was a risky place to be. The relations between Tibet and British India were not good. Every Indian was thought to be a British spy. Swami Akhandananda himself was also suspected. The lamas were once about to kill him when one of them intervened saying, 'He is a mere boy, let him go.' Soon the lamas became very friendly. Undoubtedly here also his monastic qualities helped to bring him close to the lamas.

Once some lamas decided to visit India and invited Swami Akhandananda to join them. He gladly agreed.

When they reached Almora, it so happened that Swami Shivananda was there. The two brother-disciples embraced each other and began to cry. Swami Shivananda said, 'Brother, it's hard to believe that you're alive. All this is by the grace of the Lord. We all thought you were dead.'

After Swami Akhandananda reached Calcutta, his next plan was to go to the Himalayas again and cross over into central Asia. He started walking. Following the course of the Ganges, he came to the village of Mahula in the district of Murshidabad. Here he saw a sight which made him stop. A little girl was weeping. He asked her, 'Mother, why are you weeping?' The story the girl narrated was this: Her mother had sent her to fetch some water and she had come to the market-place with their only earthen pitcher. She filled it with water from the tubewell and was carrying it back when it slipped from her hands and broke into pieces. She did not know how to face her mother. She would beat her mercilessly, but the worst thing was that they had no money to buy another pitcher.

Swami Akhandananda bought another pitcher for the girl who stopped crying and started for home. But Swami Akhandananda soon found himself surrounded by a crowd of hungry children. They were crying, 'Give us food, we are starving.'

Swami Akhandananda discovered that the whole area was in the grip of a terrible famine. But what could he do, he himself a beggar? From the Swami's great heart came the answer. Through his unremitting efforts, and those of his brother monks who came later, today, 100 years later, there is in that area, at Sargachhi, a Ramakrishna Ashrama complete with a high school, a dispensary, a library and a network of welfare centres in the surrounding villages.

THE WORLD WE LIVE IN

The question is, do we know the kind of world we live in? Sometimes we feel we know all about it; sometimes we feel we know nothing about it. It is like a puzzle, and we are at a loss to know how to tackle it.

But this is not the only problem. Another problem, a bigger problem, is that we do not know ourselves. What are we aiming at? And what are the means we are going to employ to get there? Somehow or other, we have made a mess of everything. If we have made a mess of ourselves, it is because of our ignorance. Because we are ignorant, we are vain. Because we are vain, we are not able to see our shortcomings. We are brutes in human form. We are selfish, mean, and wicked. We boast of our science and technology. But how do we use them? Do we use them to fight poverty and disease, or to destroy innocent lives? The question has to be faced and an answer found to the question.

We have fought shy of the question a long time, but the time has come when we must call a spade a spade. We have vast resources, but do we use them the way they should be used? The question of all questions is how advanced countries use their resources. Do they not use them to increase their military power? Is there not an arms race going on all the time behind the scenes? Not only that, some of the nations are trading in arms to make money for themselves and to help friendly nations to acquire arms so that they may use them against a common enemy. Between the countries there is no love or goodwill, there is instead suspicion and distrust. One nation competes with another for power and supremacy. There is always the threat of a war breaking out. Likewise, these nations would like to save money for food, health, and education, but the international situation compels them to use their resources otherwise. As a result, there is no peace between the nations. There is also no progress in health, education, and culture. The smaller nations are not free to decide what they should do. They act as the bigger nations dictate.

What the world needs today is good leadership. We have now leaders who think of the interests of their own countries, but hardly ever of the rest of the world. These leaders do not realize that they have to take a holistic view of things. The world is one and so also is mankind. A good leader must be a leader of the world as a whole. He is concerned for every country, small or big, friendly or hostile. He would like to see a new philosophy of life pursued in the world, a philosophy which tells everybody to live for others. Selfishness is a crime which can hardly be forgiven.

We talk of progress, but what is progress? How is it to be judged? Is it merely physical well-being? No doubt it includes physical well-being, but, more important, it is moral excellence. Anybody without an urge for moral excellence is dying, if not already dead. If we have to have a better world, first and foremost, we have to be better men and women. It is the leaders who have to show us the way to be better men and women. Leadership does not mean only political leadership; it means also moral and cultural leadership. The world will never be a better one until and unless we have better men and women. By 'better' men and women we mean men and women better in moral and cultural qualities. Progress means progress in more human qualities.

GOD AND MAN

How are God and man related to each other? Are they poles apart? Some people say they are different, but the difference is only in degree and that it is possible for them to come close to each other. But what does this mean? Does this mean that man can be like God? Is that possible? Is such a suggestion not an insult to God?

It is difficult to say what God is like. He is almighty, unique, and supreme. There can be no comparison between God and man. There is nothing like God. All that exists is subservient to him.

No doubt man is subservient to Him, but does that mean that man has no will of his own? Is he like a plaything in the hands of God? To what extent can man determine his fate?

There is much debate about this. Some people say man can do nothing unless God approves it. Others say man can do whatever he likes. Whatever the truth may be, the tussle between man and God is more imaginary than real. Wise people suggest that we completely surrender to God. Not that we need not work hard. We shall certainly work hard, but at the same time we shall leave everything in the hands of God. What God decides is the best for us.

How is it that some people love God, depend on Him, and are happy despite the fact that they do not get what they want? These people are honest, simple, and are happy with whatever they have. They do not blame God if they do not get what they want. Rather, they think they did not deserve what they wanted. Some of them even think it is for their own good that God denies them what they pray for.

The relationship between God and man varies from one individual to another. Each individual has his own concept of God, and it is this concept that determines his relationship with God. It is out of this concept that grows what is called religion. Religion gives people a sense of unity. It is a way that they can follow together to reach a given goal. Loosely speaking, God is the name of that goal. It is a state that man tries to attain, hoping it will give him peace and happiness.

Religion is not magic. It is hard work, but, at the same time, it makes you feel you are getting closer to God. How does this happen? You change. And this change is in the mind. You feel you have more self-control than ever before and you are a better individual in all respects. It is this change that makes all the difference. Are you less selfish? Do you feel more for others than you did before? These are some of the criteria by which you judge the kind of change that is taking place within you.

Religion is a commitment to being good and doing good. People will judge your religion by what you are and what you do. True religion is not in professing a creed or dogma. True religion is a science of growth—moral and spiritual.

Religion is often condemned because of its sectarianism. Someone professes a particular religion, and he thinks his is a better religion. Not only that, he also thinks he is a superior person just because of his religion. This is not what religion is meant for. Religion is meant for spreading love, friendship, and goodwill. It should foster a sense of oneness. The world is one and all humanity is one. Religion should make us love and care for each other.

LORD KRISHNA

What is religion? There are times when people get confused about it. Right becomes wrong and wrong becomes right. It is a critical time. At this juncture, somebody appears who gives a clear idea about religion and the confusion ends. People are very happy then. Such a person is described as an Avatar, that is, an Incarnation of God. It is as if God Himself has assumed a human body and his life is an example for man to follow. Lord Krishna was one such person. He himself makes this declaration in the *Srimat Bhagavat Gita*.

The *Gita* is a remarkable book. It is the sum and substance of the vast literature known as the Upanishads. The Upanishads are like a cow, Arjuna is like a calf, and the *Gita* is like the cow's milk. The *Gita* answers any question that you may have about man and his life. The answers are clear, direct and convincing.

The book has a dramatic beginning. The Kauravas and the Pandavas are cousins who are about to begin a war over their rights. At this crucial moment, Arjuna, the chief of the Pandavas, refuses to fight. He says to fight with dear and near ones for wealth and property is wrong. He would rather live by begging than hurt his relatives. Sri Krishna, Arjuna's friend as well as charioteer, ridiculed Arjuna for his show of being a peace-loving man. He was not what he claimed he was. He bluntly called him a coward. Finally, Arjuna agreed to fight. Krishna's contention was that Arjuna must be honest with himself.

The next important issue Krishna discusses is non-attachment. He says no one can stay idle for a moment. He has to do something or other. But what will he do? According to Krishna, whatever he may do, he should not expect any results for himself. 'For God and for others'—this should be his motto. He should be *in* the world but not *of* it. His attachment must be to God and God alone, and he must also have a steady mind.

Arjuna asks him what a steady-minded man is like. According to Krishna, he is free from all desires. Good and bad, pleasure and pain—all are alike to him. He totally withdraws himself from worldly considerations. He is always one only with himself. He identifies himself with everybody and everything.

Arjuna is confused. If he has to work, how can he be quiet at the same time? Krishna says: 'Surrender everything to me.' He also cites himself as an example. He says that he works but is indifferent to the results of the work he does. He asks Arjuna to be like him, indifferent to all results. An Avatar shows us the way and we should follow it. The *Gita* is a handbook to which we may turn for guidance in our day-to-day life.

Krishna has been a popular Avatar in India. One reason for this is that he is very human. And he emphatically declares that whoever loves him will be under his protective care. He also does not insist that you follow a certain path. If you follow the path that suits you best, Krishna is pleased. You may also find in him the model of a person you would like to be.

If you look upon him as an Avatar, he is one of the best. If you think he is human, he is the best man possible. Either way, follow him.

HOW TO PRAY

Saints and seers are people who have realized God. They are immensely happy. But they are not selfish people. They want others to be happy also. If people approach them for instructions about how to realize God, they gladly teach them. One of the things the teacher asks you to do is to repeat some words. These words are called a *mantra*. 'Mantra' means the word or words by repeating which you get liberation. The mantra is secret. You are not supposed to disclose it to others.

A mantra is terse and succinct. It may consist of only one word, or it may consist of several words put together. But it has the power to completely change you as an individual. As you repeat it you gradually become completely transformed—as if you are a lump of clay and a potter is shaping you as he likes.

The question is: Where does the mantra derive its power from? It derives its power from God. The teacher realizes God, and he becomes like God Himself. And when he speaks to you, you feel as if God is speaking to you. Then he whispers a mantra to you. The mantra is the medium through which God is transmitting his power to you.

There is immense power within you, but this power is sleeping. It is like a sleeping snake. If the snake is awakened, it raises its hood and you then see what power it has. Similarly, you have to awaken the power within you. The mantra helps do this, for it comes from a person who has realized God.

The teacher gives you the mantra and tells you how you should repeat it. When you repeat the mantra, no one should hear it. The number of times you should repeat it is not important. What is important is where the mind is when you are repeating the mantra. Is the mind on God? Repeating the mantra is not a physical exercise; it means communion with God. You should then feel his presence, as if you are one with Him.

As you repeat the mantra, you should meditate on the *ishta*, the form of God that is dearest to you. God is one and the same, but devotees love to think of Him with different names and in different forms. Just as the devotees seek God, God also seeks the devotees.

There is a saying in Bengali that the 'name' and the 'named' are not different. This is why you are advised to meditate on God while repeating the mantra. If you keep practising this, you may see in a vision that the letters of the mantra have become bright and luminous, and along with it, the divine figure you have been so long meditating on. Not only that, you may also see the whole of yourself shining with light. You, the mantra, and the deity the mantra represents—all three become one. You have then reached your goal.

The mantra leads you to your goal, but it also sustains you through your troubles and sufferings. There are times when you are haunted by some thoughts. You are confused and you do not know what to do. The mantra then comes to your rescue.

If people seek God it is because they seek happiness. The mantra always keeps you in touch with God and your mind is then filled with joy and happiness. Gradually, as you go on repeating the mantra, it becomes a habit, and you soon find you are always repeating it—even in sleep. Some people *never* stop repeating the mantra. That is, they are always in the presence of God. For a seeker of God, nothing is more satisfying than this.

NOTHING TO HIDE

A holy person has to be very strict with himself. He cannot do anything wrong, in private or in public. If he is honest, he is honest always, in all circumstances. He is honest not for ovation from others; he is honest for his own sake, irrespective of what people think of him. It is not unlikely that people will misunderstand him, praising him when it is not due or blaming him for no fault of his own. But he is totally unconcerned about what people think of him. His only concern is that he is what he wants to be. People may call him mad or a saint—it is all the same to him. He is what he is.

One such person was Ramakrishna. What sort of person was he? It is safe to say he was not a normal person. But can we say he was a mad man? Turn to any page you like of his *Gospel* and you will be struck by his wit and wisdom. When he was young he hardly ever went to school, but in later days the best scholars of his time listened to him for hours together spellbound. He may have been speaking about high philosophy, but he spoke with authority and nobody contradicted him.

What was more remarkable was the kind of life he lived. He preached renunciation, but he also practised everything that he preached. He would not accept any money, nor would he accept any gift unless it was something he needed for his bare subsistence. He would not hurt anyone. He would not even react if anyone hurt him. He was love personified.

Ramakrishna had nothing to hide. He lived a life as

clear as the sun. At home or in Calcutta, he was always in public view, and he was hardly ever alone. People loved his company, and he loved theirs as much. Never before was there a holy man whose daily life was so meticulously recorded. He lived in a small room on the temple premises of Dakshineswar. As people entered the courtyard to go to the temple, they could see Ramakrishna sitting on his bed with scores of people squatting on the floor in front of him, hanging on his words. This is how M., the author of the *Gospel*, first saw him.

Religious people tend to hide what they do to realize God. And their spiritual practices, whether personal or of the Order to which they belong—are often secret. Ramakrishna, however, never hid them. His religious practices, even the most bizarre of them, were no secret. People saw what he was doing, and in later years, he himself talked about them to his disciples. He wanted his disciples to follow him, and he would be happy if they could do even a fraction of what he had done.

Ramakrishna particularly wanted his disciples to watch him and test him so that they would be sure he was not a hypocrite. He used to say, 'I have had to pass many tests.' We are thankful to those who conducted them. Dr Mahendralal Sarkar was one of those. He was a scientist, and in the beginning he was not at all impressed by Ramakrishna's ecstasies. Then one day he examined Ramakrishna in every possible way while he was in ecstasy and found no reason to doubt its genuineness. He finally accepted Ramakrishna as he was—a mystic, beyond the understanding of the ordinary world. But Ramakrishna did not care what people thought of him—whether they thought he was a god-man or a man not in his right senses. He was happy that he was what he was.

GOD'S HANDWRITING

Emerson once described beauty as God's handwriting. In what sense is beauty God's handwriting? Is it because God creates this beauty? But God creates ugly things also, doesn't he? As God is the sole creator, he is responsible for both good and bad things. Everything is his handwriting, good or bad. Why then single out beauty as God's handwriting, leaving us to guess whose handwriting ugly things can be? Are the ugly things Satan's? It is difficult to believe that there is anyone like Satan to whom everything bad or ugly can be attributed.

How then do you explain ugly things? Where do they come from and why do they exist at all? If God and Satan are two separate creators, the former creating beautiful things and the latter creating ugly things, it would appear that Satan is more powerful than God—for the number of ugly things in the world is far in excess of the number of beautiful things.

The question now arises whether or not it is possible to discriminate good things from bad. Is there any universally accepted criterion by which good can be distinguished from bad? There is none. What is good to you may not be good to another person. Not only that, what you consider to be good now you may not consider to be good at another time.

Good and bad are relative terms. They vary from one individual to another. The thing itself is always the same, but it is good or bad depending on our own tastes. Good or bad, God is the creator of both. But how can God create anything bad? Is he not always good? God is God, above good and bad. He always remains the same, untouched by time and space—by anything.

But if God 'writes' something, will he not write something good? Not necessarily. God is like the sun, giving light to be used for whatever purpose you like. You may use the light for a good purpose or for a bad purpose, just as you like. You cannot blame the sun if you do something wrong by taking advantage of the sunlight. Similarly, the sun cannot claim any credit if you do something good.

God gives you the power to do whatever you like. If you use the power for a bad purpose, it is your fault and you have to pay for it. Similarly, if you use the power to do something good, it goes to your credit and you may claim some reward for it, if you want to. God is the source of everything, good or bad. If you like something, you say it is good, and if you don't like it, you say it is bad. The same thing is good or bad according to your inclination. God has nothing to do with it.

Emerson is right when he says God's handwriting is beautiful, for whatever God does for us is an opportunity for us to improve ourselves. If we do not improve ourselves, it is our fault and not God's.

But what is good and what is bad? We are still puzzled. What is good at one moment may not be good at another. Yet it does not matter. Let us concentrate on what appears to be good now and accept it as the thing we are seeking. Very soon we will be disillusioned and will start searching for what is truly good. This search leads us to the goal of life. And it is on the milestones we have to cross during this search that we see God's beautiful handwriting.

A LEAP IN THE DARK

Is religion a leap in the dark? What guarantee is there that if you pray, your prayer will be heard, or if you sacrifice something in the name of God, you are not making the sacrifice in vain? Almost every religion asks you to practise self-restraint. Often the implication is that by so doing you are able to claim rewards in some form or other. But what if you keep defying religious injunctions? You ought to be punished, but, more often than not, you are not. The fact of the matter is that there are no hard and fast rules about what you should do and should not do. Worse, there appears to be no visible agent which tells you what is right and what is wrong, nor is there anyone to enforce the rules laid down for men to follow.

But, is religion only a matter of 'dos and don'ts'? Who frames these rules and who enforces them? If there is a God, where is He? Why can't we see Him? How does He operate? Almost every religion talks of God, but what it says about Him is vague if not altogether baseless. One common thing religion says about Him is that He is the creator of this world. If He is the creator of this world, He must then be bigger than the world. Why can't we see Him then? Where does He hide Himself? And if He is the creator of this world, who is His creator? one might ask. Just as He is called the creator of the world, He is also called its destroyer. But just as we do not see Him create anything, we do not see Him destroy anything, either. Why then do we attribute the creation and destruction of things to Him? We cannot help asking what sort of person He is.

Is He a rational person, a person concerned with things he creates? If He is concerned with things He creates, why does He destroy them? Let us say He is not answerable to anybody for what He does or does not do, He being the supreme authority. He has His own reasons for what He does or does not do, and it may be the reasons are all sound and good, though beyond our understanding. The question is: What sort of person is God? A whimsical person? A tyrant?

Man is the most intelligent of all animals. He can think, judge, and argue. He can decide what is right and wrong, good and bad. He can act individually and also collectively. He has a good memory. He remembers his past and meets his future in the light of his past. It is only man who can do this. No wonder man is said to be next to God. He alone can defy God and he does, whether for good or evil. He questions the very existence of God.

The question is: Since we do not see God, and have no convincing proof that God exists, why should we bother about Him? Is it not absurd that we should pray to a God whose very existence is in question and whose attitude towards us is not always good? This leads us to the question, if it is possible to have a religion without a God. Swami Vivekananda defined religion as 'being good and doing good'. If that definition is correct, where is the place for God? To be good and to do good you don't have to have a God to help you. God, if He exists at all, is the epitome of perfection. Try to be like Him. Even if God does not exist, perfection exists. Let us not waste time arguing about God; let us instead be 'God', that is, be perfect.

INDIA AS A COUNTRY

India is a country of saints and sages. In books on its history you read more about its holy men and women than about its kings and warriors. The real heroes in the eyes of the people are those who renounce everything for God, and not those who fight to create an empire. By this token, Buddha is the greatest hero, to be loved and worshipped for all time. There are others also, though perhaps not as great. They too are remembered and loved. They are people who fought with the spirit and not with the sword. They showed us the way to conquer our self and be happy, for happiness is everybody's goal of life. If we are happy, we can make others happy also—not only the members of our family, but everybody we deal with.

But how was Buddha, who was penniless and homeless, a happy person? If that is the criterion for being happy, every beggar in the world would be happy and be a Buddha. Poverty is certainly not an ideal; rather it is a sin. It has to be avoided by all means.

India attaches more importance to moral values than to material wealth. In this country a poor but honest person is more respected than a rich but dishonest person. 'Truth above everything else'—this is India's motto. Your character is more important than anything else—more important than money, scholarship, social status, and so on. From this, people think India is other-worldly. That is not correct. India believes life has a purpose and that purpose is the search for perfection. Be perfect by all means—this is what India says. Money, power, fame—all these are trash. What you are as a person is what counts. If you are a person who feels for other people, who is prepared to make any sacrifice necessary for the sake of others, you are indeed a great person by Indian standards.

It would be a mistake if it is thought that India advocates escapism. India preaches nothing of the sort. India asks you to enjoy life, but enjoy it with discretion. Enjoy whatever you want, but in a limited way. Self-restraint is the keynote of the Indian way of life. Never give up to temptation. If you are reckless in your enjoyment, you end up being swallowed by what you are trying to enjoy.

It is not India's intention to be a killjoy. She may say that every moment of life should be well utilized, but this does not mean that life has to become a torture. India's outlook on life is best seen in her fine arts. Everything India does is worship. Nothing is secular to her. God is everywhere and in everything. Softness, amiability, goodwill for all—these are hallmarks of the Indian character. These are not weaknesses; these are the results of her love of God, of human beings, of everything in the world. India believes in friendliness towards all. This is not weakness; this is a sign of her large heart. India has welcomed races from everywhere. Nowhere else do you see so many races, languages, and religions. People live together, and, on the whole, live in peace and harmony. The rest of the world may think that Indians are cowardly. This is a mistake. There was a time when India could have conquered her neighbouring countries, but this is not India's way.

VEDANTA IN PRACTICE

Is it possible to practise Vedanta in everyday life? Our teachers will say, 'Yes, it is possible.' Not only that, they will say that you must practise it daily, every moment of your life—in your thought, speech, and action. Nothing can be better than that—a person so transformed that he sees God everywhere and in everything. This is the essence of Vedanta.

Vedanta says you are God Himself, you are one with everything, you are one with the whole universe. You are happy if everybody else is happy; you are unhappy if a single person in the world is unhappy. You are one with all and all are one with you.

Vedanta is a matter of being, something you experience and you cannot share with others. It is a conviction which is your own and which changes you altogether—body and mind both. You experience it as an individual, but the experience is something unique, something not given to many. And as a result of this experience, you become a person who is spotless in character. You love the entire humanity as your own. There is nobody who is hostile to you. Each individual is a friend, a relation whose well-being is yours.

Is it possible to grow up with an outlook which learns to treat the entire human race as one? Surely we are different from one another in race and religion. This difference is natural. But can we not still live with one another in peace? Why can't we at least follow the principle of 'live and let live'? Let us differ from one another. Vedanta teaches 'unity in diversity'. We cannot all be the same. We are bound to differ. We grow best when we are free. We need a world where there is love and goodwill for everybody.

Vedanta envisages such a world. We are not trying to have a world where there is uniformity. We are trying to have unity in the midst of diversity. It is One that appears to be many. It is one single Self that appears to be many by virtue of its separate superimpositions. A boy wears different masks and he looks different: sometimes like a monkey, sometimes like a dog, and sometimes like a cat. The boy is the same, but because of his masks he looks different.

Similarly, there is one single Existence in the world, but this same Existence looks different because of its different names and forms. Our delusion is that we take these names and forms to be real, and we take the one Existence to be many, according to the names and forms we attribute to it. It is one single Self that bears many names. It is like one single person standing in a room with many mirrors. There seems to be many persons, but this is an illusion. There is, in reality, only one.

As a student of Vedanta, how would you behave in your day-to-day life? You would see yourself in everybody else. You would treat everybody as your own and would make no distinction between yourself and others. Caste, country, religion—all these make no difference to you. All are one and the same to you.

But has there ever been anybody who was able to treat all alike—to treat himself and others as the same? There was Buddha. There was Ramakrishna. All were the same to them. They showed us what Vedanta is like in practice.

DOES GOD EXIST ?

Many people say that God does not exist. If God exists, they argue, why should there be any unfairness? Why should good people suffer while bad people prosper? And why is there no proof that God exists?

But if God does exist, does He interfere if there is something wrong somewhere? Can it be said that He interferes in favour of those who are good and against those who are bad? It is difficult to say whom God supports—the strong or the weak. Why are there natural calamities that take a heavy toll of life? Why are there wars? What is the role of God in defining human destiny? Why do people pray to God? Does prayer help? Then if God exists, how much is He responsible for a person's destiny or for what happens to the world?

There are two distinct ways of looking at this problem: One, you hold God responsible for everything that happens; and another, God may or may not exist, but we ourselves are responsible for everything that happens to us, good or bad. We will not bring in God.

The latter view holds nature responsible for natural calamities. Gandhiji blamed the people of Bihar for the earthquake that took a heavy toll of life in 1934. He said God punished them this way because they practised caste. But Tagore pooh-poohed the idea. He said nature was responsible for the calamity, and that neither God nor human beings had anything to do with it.

But the people who believe that God is responsible

for everything say that He creates as well as destroys. He is almighty. He can change things as He likes. He is the source of everything good and pleasant. But then the question arises, who creates the bad and unpleasant things?

There are again people who think that, just as there is one called God who is the source of everything good, there is another called Satan who is the source of everything bad. God and Satan are always fighting each other. They are fighting through one individual and another, and they are also fighting through one country and another. Good and evil, they say, are two opposite forces, always fighting each other.

Is there any way of bringing about peace between these opposite forces? Not unless we recognize that our mutual well-being lies in peace and harmony. Whether we believe in God or not, whether we believe in a Satan or not, we cannot exterminate one another. Like it or not, we have to live together. Not only that, we also have to share whatever we have, and we have to love and care for each other. Our well-being lies in our being together.

Separateness in any sense is not desirable. We cannot be, and do not want to be, separate from one another. We may differ in terms of language, faith, or complexion. These differences are superficial. We are one in Spirit, in our being. We have common problems and we will fight those problems together. Whether we believe in God or not, we are divine when we are all one. And what we need is to manifest the divinity which is within us, lying dormant.

Of course God exists, and because He exists there are plenty of good men and women all over the world. Let us make use of them as best we can.

WHOM TO FOLLOW?

The question is, who are our ideals, and who are the people we should follow? Shall we follow people like Buddha and Christ of the past, and Ramakrishna and Gandhi of more recent times? Is that possible? Or more to the point, is that desirable? Are they not out of place in the present-day world? Certainly they were great men in their time, but judged by current standards, they would seem to be anachronisms. How can you expect the younger generation to follow them? Isn't it insulting to ask them to follow those people of days long gone?

Are there not any qualities in Buddha or Gandhi which are still relevant? Take one example—the quality of honesty, for instance. A person of any generation would feel proud to be known as honest. Honesty is a quality of the highest value for anyone to aspire to. It does not matter when and in what circumstances you practise it. Whatever the situation, you command respect from all around you when you are recognized as honest. And it is not that you seek this respect. People automatically love and respect you because you are honest.

But whether people love and respect you or not, you are honest, because you cannot help but be honest. It is part of your nature to be honest, and that is why you are so. You are honest not because you are seeking a reward or trying to escape a punishment. You are honest because you are honest. You are what you are, irrespective of everything.

Buddha died long ago, but many people still remember

him, love him, and worship him. They love to think of him—of his life and character. They think of him as an ideal person, and they want to be like him in every way. And because they love him, they even worship his image. Though he is no longer alive, they worship his image as if it is a living being. They offer him food and drink— everything he would have liked if he were alive. Why? Because they want to be transformed into a Buddha. But the transformation they want is not a physical transformation. They want to change themselves in terms of life and character. They want to acquire Buddha's love of peace, his humility, his selflessness, and, above everything else, his self-restraint.

Over the centuries there have been people who have tried to be like Buddha. But some of them have only taken notice of the externals—that is, they have merely changed superficially. Basically they have remained the same men and women. This is futile. If you want to imitate Buddha, then imitate his life and character. Try to make your whole being a Buddha.

What is religion for? It is to change our life and character. We want to be better people. A better person is one who is honest, good, kind, and is ready to help others without asking for anything in return. If Buddha is the ideal, let us be like Buddha at any cost. If by worshipping an image of Buddha we can become like Buddha, what is wrong there? What is important is to be a Buddha.

Let us be prepared to follow anything or anybody, provided it helps us become as good a person as, say, Buddha or Christ. Choose whomever you like. The choice is not that important. Being is important, being the person you have chosen to follow.

TOTA PURI

Tota Puri was a monk who belonged to a non-dualistic order. No one knows for certain where he was born or who his teacher was. But what we do know is that he was a wandering monk who spent most of his time meditating. The only language he spoke was Hindi; at least, he did not know Bengali. What attracted him to Bengal is a matter of conjecture. Perhaps he wanted to have a bath in the Bay of Bengal and then pay a visit to Puri, a common practice among Hindu monks.

But what attracted him to Dakshineswar is difficult to tell. Was it Sri Ramakrishna? There is no evidence that he had heard of Sri Ramakrishna. True, Sri Ramakrishna was becoming known among English-educated people of Calcutta, but at that time the number of people who had heard of him was minimal. Yet if you look closely at the course of events following Tota Puri's arrival at Dakshineswar, you would feel tempted to conclude that everything had been pre-planned.

At any rate, Tota Puri's meeting Sri Ramakrishna proved a turning-point in the religious history of India. After that, religion was no longer a sectarian belief. It became an all-embracing outlook rising far above narrow beliefs and prejudices. Tota Puri taught no creed or dogma. He taught Vedanta, which is nothing but Truth—the essence of the Eternal.

When Tota Puri arrived at Dakshineswar and got off the boat, he found himself in the midst of people of all classes. Among them, there was one who caught his eye.

He was extraordinary. This was Sri Ramakrishna. Tota took him aside and said : 'Look, I can see in you great spiritual possibilities. I can help you fulfil them. But I can't stay here for long. I can only stay for three days.' Sri Ramakrishna replied : 'I don't know anything. I will have to ask my mother.'

Tota thought Sri Ramakrishna meant his human mother, but when he found Sri Ramakrishna going into the temple to ask Mother Kali, he was shocked. To him Mother Kali was nothing but a piece of stone. That an intelligent human being would seek the advice of a piece of stone on such an important matter was beyond his imagination. When Sri Ramakrishna came out of the temple, Tota was curious to know what his 'Mother' had said. Sri Ramakrishna told him : 'Mother has approved the idea. She says she has brought you here just for this.' Tota Puri did not know what to make of it. He must have felt immensely amused! He began to like this disciple. But where his 'Mother' was concerned, he did not know what to think.

Not much is known of what passed between the teacher and the disciple. It was a world into which there was no access for a third person. But before this, Tota Puri had never spent more than three days at any place. Yet he spent eleven months at Dakshineswar. This was because he loved his disciple. He loved him because he found his disciple had not only grasped Vedanta fully, but had also learnt its practical implications. Vedanta had so long been a theory to him. Tota now learnt how Vedanta could—and should—be used in day-to-day life. Vedanta teaches that everything is divine. Even a piece of stone is divine. It is this idea which the teacher learnt from the student. The roles between them had reversed.

MANI

Among the many names the author of *The Gospel of Sri Ramakrishna* used in order to hide his identity, his favourite was 'Mani'. Why did he want to hide his identity, and why was 'Mani' his favourite pseudonym? Those who knew him well say that he was very shy. Sri Ramakrishna once scolded him because he would not dance. But shyness about dancing and shyness about disclosing one's identity are not the same kind of shyness. It is difficult to guess why the author wanted to remain anonymous.

In fact, he always avoided the use of the words 'I' and 'mine', like his Master did. His students said he always walked with a finger on his lips, which suggested he did not want you to talk. In fact, M. hardly ever talked unless he had to. His students and colleagues also said he had the habit of retiring to a solitary corner on the roof of the school building and silently reading a notebook. If anyone asked him what he was reading, he would invariably refuse to answer. His close friends, however, had no difficulty in guessing that he was reading his diary with the notes of his Master's conversations.

But even those who were very close to him were not able to have a look at the diary. Once Girish Ghosh, the noted dramatist, said to M.: 'I hear you have noted down the conversations of our dear Master in your diary. Why don't you let us have a look at them? Or why don't you publish them in some journal? These conversations are for the benefit of the whole world.'

Holy Mother was perhaps the first person who had the

privilege of hearing the diary read out. Later, she wrote to M. saying that as she heard the diary, she felt she was hearing the Master speaking to her. No tribute could be higher than this, nor could there be a better testimony. When the first volume of the *Gospel* appeared, it was an immediate success.

M., the man, however, remained the same—shy, soft-spoken, and humble. In conduct he was more like a child (Mani) than an old man. He had chosen an apt name for himself—Mani. In later days, he lived alone on the roof of a school building, which he owned. In the evening a group of people would come and join him for the evening vespers. After that they would meditate together for a while. M., with his long white beard, looked like an ancient sage just come down from the Himalayas.

As time passed, more people gathered. They kept looking at him, hoping he would say something. But no one dared break the silence. Finally M. himself spoke. He asked what day it was. Someone answered, and M. then began to say why the day was important to him. 'On this day,' he said, 'Sri Ramakrishna visited Balaram Basu's house. He had asked me also to come, and so I did. There were a few other devotees also. The Master started singing, and he also danced. He asked everyone to join him. Others did, but I did not. I was too shy to dance. He wanted me to sing and dance with abandon, but I could never bring myself to dance. I sang, of course, but always in a low voice.'

M. remained a shy man to the last day of his life. Nevertheless, he was a person to reckon with. He was not a monk, but he influenced many young men to embrace monasticism. As regards the *Gospel*, it will remain forever a monument to his memory.

TRADITION

How much does a tradition count in one's life? It depends upon how you have been brought up. Most people judge something to be right or wrong according to the traditions which have shaped their life and character. If you are in a dilemma, for instance, you know almost at once what you should or should not do. You do not have to think a long time about it because you have been brought up amidst certain traditions, and they are traditions which taught you to do what is right. As a result, you judge things almost by instinct and you never make a mistake.

Traditions are things you learn from people you live with. For the most part you learn from your parents. Here, the proverb 'Example is better than precept' is most important. In ancient India, children were taught to look upon their parents as God: 'Matri devo bhava, pitri devo bhava—treat your mother as God; treat your father as God'—this was the lesson they were given. As a result, parents were well looked after to the last day of their life. Three generations lived together and were happy. It was their traditions that bound them together with love and affection. What we need now are traditions which will teach us to love and care for others.

If we do not learn certain qualities from our traditions—qualities such as humility, mutual love and respect, and selflessness—where shall we learn them? Traditions are ways of life which shape our life-style. Each family has a distinct way of life which it passes from one generation to another. It is not that the members of the family teach each other how to behave. They are together and they learn from one another what to do and how to do it. But rarely are they taught verbally. They learn by observing. They observe each other and learn what they should and should not do. They thus learn to fix a standard which they maintain in their dealings with one another. Similarly, each individual, family, or society fixes a standard to maintain in personal or collective life.

Just as each family has its traditions, similarly, each country also has its traditions. A civilization is nothing but the traditions which are passed down from one generation to another. True progress in a civilization means progress in attitudes of mutual love and goodwill. Progress is not just in clothes and comforts. Let us have such progress. But unless material progress is joined with progress in qualities of the heart, civilization is without any foundation.

Traditions change. They change because life itself changes. But it is wrong to think that the change is always for the better. Sometimes circumstances force on us things we do not like, and sometimes we discard traditions which we once valued. This is suicidal, yet we are infatuated by new things, and therefore we throw away the best in our heritage.

The best thing to do is to cherish our traditions, even if this means cherishing things which have outlived their utility. Things we do not need will die out automatically. But we need not be in a hurry to replace old things just because they are old. Maybe they appear out of place in the context of our present-day life, but if we look closely we will find their intrinsic merit is still intact. We should respect our old traditions even if we are not able to live up to them.

MOTHER OF ALL

Once Sarada Devi entered Sri Ramakrishna's room at Cossipore. Sri Ramakrishna was ill; in fact, he was dying. Mother looked at him and understood that he wanted to say something but was hesitating to say it. She asked: 'Why don't you speak out what you have to say?' Sri Ramakrishna had difficulty speaking. Still, with great strain, he said: 'I am doing all I can for the good of humanity, but don't you think you also owe something to humanity to help people realize the goal of their life? Look at the people of Calcutta. They seem to have forgotten the purpose of life. They live as if the purpose of life is only to enjoy sense pleasure. Do something for them. Else why did you come?'

Mother replied: 'But who am I? A mere woman. What can I do?' Sri Ramakrishna smiled and said: 'What will you do? You will do much more than what I have done. Compared to what you will do, I have done nothing.'

Sri Ramakrishna's prediction came true. After his passing away, Mother Sarada Devi took over his role, more unconsciously than consciously. For the remaining thirty-four years of her life, she taught human beings the way Sri Ramakrishna wanted. She taught not so much by words as by being what Sri Ramakrishna was and what Sri Ramakrishna wanted her to be.

For some years after Sri Ramakrishna's passing away, Mother lived a hard and lonely life at Kamarpukur. She often had difficulty managing to get even one meal a day. No one bothered to enquire how she was maintaining herself. The monastic disciples of Sri Ramakrishna had very little contact with her. They were in the Himalayas or elsewhere, practising meditation as their Master had taught them. And Mother herself was the last person to let anybody know of her hardships. When her mother heard of her Saru's (Mother's nickname) hardships, she sent word, asking her to come and live with her. From then on Mother lived mainly at her native village, Jayrambati, or in Calcutta.

Once when Mother was visiting Bodh Gaya with some devotees, she was struck by the contrast in living conditions between these monks and the young men who had left home under the inspiration of Sri Ramakrishna. She prayed to the Master: 'When are my sons going to have a place to stay? They are spread out all over the country and live by begging. Can't they have a roof over their heads?' Once Swamiji described her as 'the Mother of the Order' (*Sangha Janani*). With tears in his eyes, he narrated the debt that the Ramakrishna Order owed to her. He said that when most of their so-called friends had deserted them, she alone stood by them.

Sarada Devi used to say that she was the Mother of all. Good or bad, rich or poor, man or animal—everybody was her child. If Mother called, a bird or a cat or a calf would answer. She would say, 'Amzad is my son just as Sarat [Swami Saradananda] is my son.' Amzad was an ill-famed criminal, whereas Sarat was a highly respected monk. She always wore a veil, but behind that veil there was a mother who loved all human beings as her children.

Sri Ramakrishna was right when he said that Mother would do more for humanity than he had done. Mother stands out as a model for the whole world to follow. She lived religion.

THE GURU

Once a guru appeared in a suburb of a town and, for one reason or another, he began to attract hordes of people. There was nothing very attractive about the man. He was short, soft-spoken, but he had a ready wit that made laughter irresistible. Two middle-aged men used to pass that way every day. They were good friends, and both had nothing but contempt for religion. They laughed as the crowd of religious seekers grew larger.

One day they sought an interview with the monk, their intention being to prove that he was a humbug. The monk welcomed them, and they asked: 'Why does a person have to have a guru? What is your role, besides exploiting innocent people?' The monk turned to one of the men and said: 'Let's say you are learning music. Why do you have to have a teacher?' Then, turning to the other man, he said: 'Or let's say you are learning homeopathy. What makes you choose a senior doctor as your teacher?' He then added, 'In both cases you have a teacher because it helps to have one.'

The two men were aghast hearing this. One of them was a student of music and the other of homeopathy. Both had teachers. Moreover, they each studied the subject the monk had spoken to them about. The two men could not explain this coincidence. They thought the monk possessed some supernatural power. They fell at his feet and begged to be accepted as his disciples.

No one knows for certain whether the monk possessed any supernatural power or not, or if he had attained something through his spiritual practices. But the fact remains that the purpose of religion is not to acquire any supernatural power. The only thing one should acquire is love of God. Love of God is also love of Truth. Religion is the way to God—that is, Truth. Religion does not mean magic. It means hard work, practice of self-control, and total rejection of ease and comfort. It does not mean love for yourself. It means love for others without expecting anything in return.

Religion is a science, a science of being. You tell yourself what you want to be and you become it. You become it not by a fluke, but by hard work. If there has been one Buddha, there may be many Buddhas. It is only a question of hard work, determination, and ceaseless effort.

You are fortunate if you have a good teacher. He shows you the way and also warns you about the temptations on the path. The teacher is himself a perfect man, and he shows you how you also can be perfect.

You are entitled to teach if you have realized what you are teaching. A blind man cannot lead another blind man. If he tries to lead anyone, he will only lead him to a disaster. In religious matters it is difficult to find a good teacher. Who is a good teacher? One who has realized the Truth. Religion is a matter of realization. It completely transforms you. You are no longer the person you once were. Your outlook changes. You see God everywhere and in everything. You see God in yourself and you also see God in every being.

The teacher helps you to become divine. But he does not teach by talking. He teaches by being. He is an example of what he wants you to be.

HOLY PLACES

All religions have their holy places. They are all over the world. The most important is the birthplace of the founder of a religion. Take the case of Buddha. He was born in Lumbini in Nepal. Naturally Lumbini is the holiest of all holy places as far as Buddhism is concerned. From all over the world Buddhists, and even non-Buddhists, pour in to pay homage to Buddha at Lumbini.

But it is not only the birthplace of Buddha which is regarded as a holy place. Gaya, where Buddha attained *nirvana* is also a holy place to Buddhists and non-Buddhists alike. Yet another holy place to the Buddhists is Sarnath, near Benaras, where Buddha set in motion his wheel of *dharma*. It is also possible to identify places, some more holy than others, where Buddha either performed a miracle or did something else of great religious significance. These places inspire us in spite of the years that have passed since he lived.

Like the places connected with Buddha, there are places which remind us of another great soul, Christ. Christ was born in Bethlehem, and every year people visit that place to pay homage to the Master. They come by the thousands. They come because they are reminded of his life and his words. He is very much alive to people.

Another Prophet is Mohammed. Like Christ, Mohammed had a hard life. He also shared the same surroundings, the desert. Even their messages had much in common. Christ was killed by people who should have worshipped him. Notwithstanding their cruelty, Jesus blessed them. Mohammed had to wage a war to restore peace in the country. He suffered much in the process, but he succeeded in handing over to his people a way of life which has held them together against all kinds of untoward situations. Every year many thousands of pilgrims visit Mecca to remember him.

Of all religions, Hinduism probably has the most number of holy places. And if you go to any holy place of the Hindus you are fascinated. Not that you see the same things you see in the holy places of Buddhism, Christianity, or Islam. The things you see in the holy places of the Hindus may be different. Nevertheless, they inspire you to love God above everything else.

The fact of the matter is that God is one and the same in all religions. Not only that, religion in its essence is one and the same—no matter by what name you call it. You may visit a holy place not of your religion, yet you will feel inspired all the same. Sometimes you may not even know you are visiting a holy place, but the place will inspire you. Sri Ramakrishna went into ecstasy when he visited Sri Chaitanya's birthplace. It was the ecstasy which made him conscious that he was on the spot where Sri Chaitanya was born.

It is a pity that many holy places are not well preserved. However that may be, a holy place is a holy place, and it has its power intact. It inspires you in the same way that it inspired your ancestors.

> The Ganges, Shiva, and Kashi: Where this Trinity is watchful, no wonder here is found the grace that leads one on to perfect bliss.—*Kashi Khanda* 35. 7-10.
>
> (In, *Banaras, City of Light*, by Diana Eck.)

A FEW DOS AND DON'TS
ACCORDING TO THE BIBLE

The Bible has several significant things to say about our daily life and habits. Take, for instance, prayer. The Bible tells us to pray quietly, with all our heart, and without drawing people's notice. Prayer is something between you and God, a silent and deep communion between yourself and your Lord.

Jesus suggests that we pray like this:

'Our Father in heaven,
hallowed be your name.
Your kingdom come,
your will be done,
on earth as it is in heaven.'

We are all in a hurry to judge others. This is too bad. This is why God says, 'Do not judge, or you too will be judged.' Not only that, you will be judged by the same yardstick that you judge others. We look at the speck of sawdust in the eyes of others, while we pay no attention to the plank in our own eye. Though we should be removing the plank from our own eye, we are much too busy trying to remove the speck from the eye of our neighbour.

We should ask, and then we will get whatever we want. We have to knock, and then the door will be opened. If we ask for bread, we may expect to get bread, but we must first ask ourselves what it is we really want. Otherwise, how can we expect to get what we want? Also, give to others what you want others to give to you. Give and take—that is the law.

Give to the poor whatever you can, but give it as

secretly as possible. Also, give it without expecting a reward—either here on earth or in heaven. Give without letting your left hand know what your right hand gives.

We may go on repeating, 'O Lord,' but that will not take us to heaven. We have to do what the Lord wants us to do. The way to God is the way to Truth. There is no easy way to God.

Let us obey God always and in all circumstances. That is how we build our house on a rock. If we do otherwise, the rain will come, the winds will blow, and our house will collapse.

Jesus taught all this from the top of a mountain, and this is why it is known as 'the Sermon on the Mount.' It is the essence of what Christ wanted to teach. Christ taught things few prophets did. He said, 'Love your enemies and pray for those who persecute you'—both very odd, indeed. But the way to God is like that—very difficult.

You are the salt of the earth. But if the salt is no longer saline, what will you do? Can you make salt saline again? No. You throw it away and people trample on it. It is lost for good.

But if you are the light of the world, you cannot be hidden. You are put on a stand and you shed light throughout the house. Be like that. Do good deeds. People will come to know and praise you. You, in your turn, will always praise God.

Every good tree bears good fruit. Every tree that does not bear good fruit is cut down and thrown into the fire. How do you distinguish a good tree from a bad one? By the fruit it bears. How do you distinguish a good man from a bad one? By his character. But you do not kill the bad man. You love him. Love him so that the good qualities in him begin to manifest.

VEDANTA :
A RELIGION OR A PHILOSOPHY ?

Vedanta is both a religion and a philosophy, depending on how you treat it. It is a religion if you think of it as a belief—a belief with all its paraphernalia. It is a philosophy if you have an original thought about life, about the world, about everything. If you think of Vedanta as a religion, you are more concerned about its practices. Also, it controls everything you say or do. What you are as an individual is more important than what your community is like.

But it is possible to practise Vedanta as a religion and a philosophy both at the same time. If you practise it as a religion, your habits and ways of life are distinctive, and people around know what sort of person you are. But the question is, do you mean what you say? If you practise what you profess, you will then be, first and foremost, honest. A Vedantin is a seeker of Truth. Truth is like God to him. He is honest in thought, speech, and action. But a Vedantin is not the only one committed to Truth. Everybody who professes to be religious is honest. As a matter of fact, Truth is religion and religion is Truth.

Vedanta recognizes only Truth. According to Vedanta, Truth is the source of everything. It is Truth from which everything emerges and it is Truth into which everything finally disappears. Vedanta also says that Truth alone exists and nothing else. Truth is one and the same, but it assumes various names and forms. The diversity we see in the world is nothing but a superimposition. If we think the superimposition is real, it is nothing but ignorance.

In the dark, you see a snake where there is a rope. But if you get a lamp, you will then see there is no snake; there is only a rope. Similarly, the whole world is a superimposition. We think it is real and it will always last. It is unfortunate that we think this. We see death all around us, yet we think we will never die. Why? Because of ignorance. Somehow or other we have to get rid of this ignorance. In fact, the goal of our life is to get rid of this ignorance.

Vedanta says there is only one single existence in this world, and that existence is known as 'Truth' (*Sat*). It is also known as 'Consciousness' (*Chit*) and 'Bliss' (*Ananda*). Our real identity is this *Sat-Chit-Ananda*. This is our Self (Atma). This Self was never born and will never die. It is always one and the same.

Vedanta says that the Self is one, but it has different names and forms. It further says that we have to love each other, for by loving others we are loving ourselves. This oneness is the keynote of Vedanta. Call it religion or philosophy, Vedanta shows us how to find unity in the midst of the diversity that surrounds us. It constantly reminds us of our unity. There is diversity, but that diversity is only in names and forms and it is temporary, superficial, and false. If we are to have a happy society, we have to make this idea of unity the root of everything we do or think.

Whether we think of Vedanta as a religion or a philosophy, it is the same. It is something that involves our whole day-to-day life—our thought, speech, and action. In short, it is something that concerns our character, our whole being.